EVOLUTIONISM: APE-MAN, BATMAN, CATWOMAN AND OTHER EVOLUTIONARY FANTASIES

(The Truth About Ape-Men — The Rest of the Story)

Volume X
Creation Science Series

By Dennis G. Lindsay

Published by
Christ For The Nations, Inc.
P.O. Box 769000
Dallas, TX 75376-9000

Printed 1995
©1995
Christ For The Nations, Inc.
All Rights Reserved
All Scripture NIV unless otherwise noted.

FOREWORD

The purpose of the Creation Science Series is simply to make information available to all laypersons interested in the subject. My intent is to provide documentation for Creation Science that is easy to read and comprehend, while eliminating much of the technical jargon that only a specialist would appreciate. For those desiring additional information from professionals in the Creation Science community, the following outstanding organizations should be contacted:

MASTER BOOKS
9260 Isaac St., Suite E
Santee, CA 92071 USA

INSTITUTE FOR CREATION RESEARCH
2100 Greenfield Dr.
Box 2667
El Cajon, CA 92021 USA

BIBLE - SCIENCE ASSOCIATION
P.O. Box 33220
Minneapolis, MN 55433-0220 USA

CREATION SCIENCE MINISTRIES
P.O. Box 6330
Florence, KY 41022 USA

CREATION EVIDENCES MUSEUM
Box 309
Glen Rose, TX, USA 76043

GENESIS INSTITUTE
7232 Morgan Ave S.
Richfield, MN 55423 USA

APOLOGETICS PRESS, INC.
230 Landmark Drive
Montgomery, AL 36117-2752

Cover design by Don Day.
Illustrations by Camille Barnes, Diane Sisco and Golan Lindsay

TABLE OF CONTENTS

Introduction:
    What's All This Monkey Business? 7

PART I: APE-MAN: FACT OR FICTION

1   The Battle for the King of
    the Anthropological Mountain 14

2   The Birth of Alien Half-Breeds. 22

3   The ABCs of Evolutionism 30

4   Alien Evolutionism 32

5   The Ape-Man Family Tree 40

6   The Missing Chain 52

7   Extinct Ape-Men Charts:
    (The Road to Fantasyland) 62

**PART II: FOUR FUNERALS FOR FOUR
EVOLUTIONARY FANTASIES
(The Rest of the Stories)**

8   The Ape-Man Syndrome 72

9   Funeral One: In Memory of Java Man
    (1891-1921) Pithecanthropus Erectus 83

10   Funeral Two: In Memory of Nebraska Man
    (1925-1927) Hesperopithecus 92

11   Funeral Three: In Memory of Nellie
    (1927-1940) Peking Man 101

12   Funeral Four: In Memory of Piltdown Man
    (1912-1953) Eoanthropus Dawsoni 108

PART III: THE NEANDERTHAL RACE

13   The Emergence of Ape-Man. 122

14	Mr. Neanderthal (1856)	124
15	The Elephant Man	133
16	Neanderthal's Relatives	136
17	A Face-Lift for the Neanderthals and a Change of Face for the Evolutionists	140
18	The Iceman of the Ice Age	147
19	Variety Within the Human Species	152

PART IV: OLDEST MAN OR FOSSIL APE (HOMOHABULUS)?

20	Skull 1470	160
21	Dating the World's Oldest Man	166
22	How Apes Become Human	170

PART V: EVOLUTIONISM'S MOST PRESTIGIOUS APE-MEN AND APE-WOMEN

23	Australopithecines (1924)	176
24	Zinjanthropus (Mr. Z) (1959)	180
25	An Ape Named Lucy — Ape-Woman of the Year	184
26	Lucy's Ludicrous Legacy Lingers On	194
27	I Love Lucy: The Ludicrous Lucy Legacy Lives On	198
28	Fossil Footprints: A Final Footnote	201
29	Evolutionism's Pagan Religion	208

PART VI: SUCCULENT SWINDLES AND DELECTABLE DECEPTIONS

30	National Geographic Society and the Stone Age Swindle	214
31	A Medley of Evolutionary Deceptions	222

| 32 | Escape from Reason | 228 |

PART VII: BIGFOOT AND OTHER ABOMINABLE CREATURES

33	Bigfoot: Fact or Fantasy?	234
34	Outcasts of Job's Day	240
35	Bigfoot of the Bible	243
36	Twenty-First Century Cavemen	247

PART VIII: THE MAKING OF MAN

37	Stone Age Mating Game: Comparative Anatomy	254
38	Kinks in the Links	267
39	The Marks of Man	276
40	The Impassable Gap	284

PART IX: APE-MAN: SPRINGBOARD FOR RACISM

41	The Roots of Racism	288
42	New Age Math: Angle + Slope = IQ?	293
43	Measuring Up to One's Brains	299
44	Sizing Up One's Cerebral Surroundings	304

PART X: THE FRAUD FROM HELL: RACISM

45	Evolutionism: Hindu Hybrid	312
46	Darwin's Delusion	318
47	Hitler and Evolutionism	322
48	Notable Evolutionists Reveal Their Bias	325
49	National Geographic Society and Racism Today	329

50	The Illusionary World of the Evolutionist	333
51	De-volution, Evil-ution and Devil-ution	339

PART XI: THE BIBLICAL PERSPECTIVE OF MAN

52	The Truth About Fred Flintstone	344
53	Dead Men Do Tell Tales	351
54	The Genesis Man	360
Conclusion		364
Endnotes		371
Bibliography		376
Illustrations		385

Introduction: What's All This Monkey Business?

Figure #1. EVOLUTIONISM'S WILDEST GUESS: TAKING A SECOND LOOK

The Emergence of Man.

Evolutionism and Scripture are in direct conflict regarding the origin of man. Evolutionists say that man has evolved from apes or some other animal form. But the Bible states that God created human beings in His own image. Did God make man or did man make God? Are we made in the image of God or is God only in man's imagination?

Monkey Theology.

Evolutionism is a fairy tale; not fact, but fantasy. The fiction began with the delusions of Darwin, who believed that man evolved out of slime. An ad in *Time* magazine promoting a *Time/Life* series entitled *The Emergence of Man* explains the evolutionary myth of man's origins.

> Today that creature who first began to raise himself above other animals no longer exists. He has become you, unique, set apart from the two million other species living on the planet by a thumb which makes your hand a precision tool, by a knee that locks you into a comfortable upright position, and by your capacity for abstract thought, and speech. All this and more has enabled your species to dominate the earth and yet you share with every other creature that ever lived the same origin. The same accident that led to

> the spontaneous generation of the first celled slimy algae three and a half billion years ago.
>
> How did it all happen? What was the evolutionary process that led to man and his conquest of a harsh and hostile environment? You will find the amazing story in *Time/Life* books new series, *The Emergence of Man.* Your introductory volume, *The Missing Link*, shows the stranger-than-science fiction world of ape-man. You will feel a sense of immediacy in visual adventure. Incredible lifelike pictorial technical photo painting.

Did you notice the phrase "pictorial technical photo paintings"? What that means is that there are no photos in the evidence of the missing link, so paintings are used to portray what the ape-man must have looked like.

Darwin tells of his delusion on page 23 of his book, *The Origin of the Species*:

> Analogy would lead me to the belief that all animals and plants are descended from one prototype ... All organic things that have ever lived on the

Earth *maybe* (italics mine) descended
by some one primordial form.

In other words, MUTATION + NATURAL SELECTION + TIME = SLIME TO MAN. SLIME TO PROTOZOA TO WORM TO FISH TO AMPHIBIAN TO REPTILE TO BIRD TO MAMMAL TO MAN. Start with nothing, add TIME and CHANCE, and amoebas become astronauts. This is nothing more than monkey mythology.

Once I was a tadpole beginning to begin,
Then I was a frog with my tail tucked in
Then I was a monkey in a banyan tree,
And now I am a professor with a Ph.D.
(Author Unknown)

How Did Man Originate? (See fig. #2.)

Did man come from Adam or apes? Did he ascend up the evolutionary ladder from goo to slime by way of the zoo until he was no longer a simian but rather a Homo sapiens? What evidence is there for missing links? What is a "missing link"? How many "missing links" make a missing chain? How many "missing links" exist today which link ape and man? How did a pig evolve from a monkey? How did one "missing link" fool the experts for over 40 years? What famous set of bones do evolutionists claims to-

Introduction: What's All This Monkey Business?

day to be the "missing link"? What is the latest evolutionary hoax? What is the biblical view of ancient man? What is the truth about bigfoot? Aren't Neanderthals considered examples of primitive ape-men? How do evolutionists determine a "missing link" to be millions of years old? What do the Bible have to say about ape-man, bigfoot and other primitive cave dwellers? What does evolutionism and racism have in common? These and other questions will be answered in this volume.

Figure #2. ARE YOU RELATED TO ADAM OR APES?

PART I
APE-MAN: FACT OR FICTION

Chapter 1: The Battle for King of the Anthropological Mountain

Chapter 2: The Birth of Alien Half-Breeds

Chapter 3: ABCs of Evolutionism

Chapter 4: Alien Evolutionism

Chapter 5: The Ape-Man Family Tree

Chapter 6: The Missing Chain

Chapter 7: Extinct Ape-Men Charts: (The Road to Fantasyland)

Chapter One

The Battle for King of the Anthropological Mountain

Figure #3. THE GREAT DEBATE: WHO'S KING OF THE MOUNTAIN?

Were You There?

Several years ago, I watched a debate on television between two of the world's leading evolutionary anthropologists (people who study ancient man). The program was entitled "You Were There." It was hosted by the distinguished media journalist and reporter, Walter Cronkite, who for many years was the anchorman for CBS' Evening World News.

The program began with Walter Cronkite holding the famous skull known as Lucy. It was discovered by Donald Carl Johanson, one of the two guests on the program. Mr. Cronkite pointed out that the dark area on the skull represented the pieces which were actually found and the light areas were where the gaps had been filled in with plaster. **(See fig. #4.)**

The camera showed a close-up shot of the skull until the two shades were unmasked. Then quickly the photographer panned away. As I reviewed this portion of the program several times, it was obvious why there was an immediate retreat from the close-up shot. The majority of the skull was filled with plaster to replace the missing pieces, including the sloping brow which monkeys tend to have. Then came a startling admission from Mr. Cronkite:

Figure #4. THE IMAGINARY APE-MAN

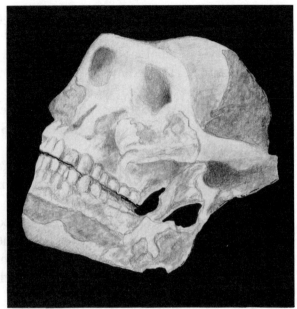

☐ **PLASTER FILL IN**
■ **ORIGINAL PIECES**

Even though we "know" man came from ape, all the bones linking man with ape found in the last 100 years would not even cover a billiards table.

Bones and Billiards.

This is astounding. To say, "Even though we

know man came from ape" suggests there is overwhelming evidence to prove such a position. But to say it knowing that the evidence collected over the last 100 years would not even cover a billiards table is beyond understanding. It suggests that those making the statement consider the listeners Neanderthals (people who are as dense as the fantasized ape-men were supposed to have been), incapable of recognizing the senselessness of such a remark.

The Battle Between Britain and the U.S.

The statement came at the beginning of the program, setting the tone for the rest of the amazing show. It was evolutionism at its "best," or, should we say, its "worst." The two featured guests were the world renowned, anthropologists, Dr. Donald Carl Johanson from the United States and Dr. Richard Leakey from England. Another war between the U.S. and Britain was about to occur.

Until the late 1970s, Dr. Leakey was king of the anthropologists as a result of his discovery of Skull 1470. This skull was considered the oldest transitional link in existence between man and ape. But all that changed in 1979 when Dr. Johanson announced to the world that "Lucy" was over one half million years older than Skull

1470. Immediately, the eyes of the evolutionary community were attracted to the beauty of this new woman in the lab. Skull 1470 now played second fiddle to Lucy.

For the next hour, the war over the planet of the apes raged on as I witnessed two adults, supposed polished men of science, act like kids as they squabbled over whose bag of bones were older and more human-like. Dr. Johanson asked Mr. Leakey to draw his time line for the ages of the two missing links in question. Leakey refused at first but finally agreed to do it. When Leakey was finished with his time line, Dr. Johanson drew a big X through it and put a question mark over it. In the background, Mr. Cronkite was smiling and quietly chuckling as he watched these two grown men act like juveniles.

Evolutionism: Still Without a Clue.

Dr. Richard Leakey stated in *National Geographic* (6/73), "Either we toss out this skull or we toss out our theories of early man." He believed that since the past theories about man's emergence were shattered by his discovery of Skull 1470, the evolutionary community doesn't have a clue as to when, where or how man ascended the ladder from the ape. The article said that Skull 1470 ruins the notion that all early fossils can be arranged in an orderly sequence of evolutionary change.

Richard Leakey stated that if he were asked to draw a family tree for man, he would have to draw a huge question mark because the evidence is too scanty to know positively man's evolutionary origin. He didn't think we would ever find the answer. **(See fig. #5.)**

The Implications of Winning.

The war of words between Dr. Leakey and Dr. Johanson was intense because each understood the implications of becoming king. Winning the gold crown meant fame and fortune with awards, grants and royalties. Although Mr. Leakey fought a good fight, Dr. Johanson won the gold and the favor of many of his colleagues. Even today many evolutionists consider Lucy to be one of the best evidences for a "missing link." However, when we take a closer look at Lucy beginning in chapter 25, we shall see that her pedigree has been forged and doesn't measure up to her image of an ape-woman. There is more to the stories of Lucy and Skull 1470, but it is not heard in the university classroom because the reputation of evolutionism is at stake. With the obvious lack of evidence for the "missing link," it would be more accurately called the missing

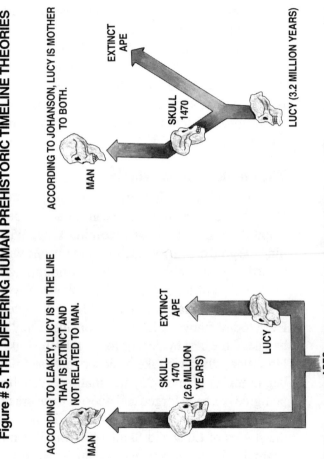

Figure # 5. THE DIFFERING HUMAN PREHISTORIC TIMELINE THEORIES

chain. Before we look at the missing chain, we shall take a look at the family tree of evolutionism and the birth of alien half-breeds.

Chapter Two

The Birth of Alien Half-Breeds

(See fig. #6.)
The ABCs of Evolutionism.

Children learn their ABCs when they are very young. Today, shortly after, they learn about the ABCs of evolutionism through mythological creatures like Ape-man, Batman, Catwoman and other fantasies. These creatures originated in evolutionists' imaginations. The film industry has capitalized on these fantasies, creating a multitude of weird and alien creatures. These creatures have become heroes and champions to youngsters. Satan has used Hollywood to spread his delusion in order to enlarge his kingdom. How is it possible that the movie industry, television and other forms of entertainment have made such a fortune from half-breeds? The answer is very simple: For decades, the evolutionary community has been charmed with the idea of the existence of such creatures. They have

Figure #6. THE ABCs OF EVOLUTIONISM AND THE ROAD TO MONKEYLAND

propagated their fantasy for more than a century, which prepared today's generation to receive and embrace the idea of alien creatures.

Who would have believed that Ninja Turtles would become a billion-dollar business and that these plastic images would be found in the homes of millions of children? For years, Superman was *the* superhero on television. Then came creatures that had the powers of Superman, but also manifested half-human and half-animal features: Batman, Catwoman and Spiderman, etc. However, these are now considered the milk toast (softcore) creatures of the industry. Hard-core creatures embody a multitude of demonic characteristics in their appearance and actions. Some of the most popular can be found in Dungeon and Dragons, which appear in comic books and video games. **(See fig. #7.)** Television video games are saturated with evil creatures of every imaginable variety and demonic shape.

These alien half-breeds have become a huge success, and children not only believe they are real, but that they have been in existence for eons. It all began in the imaginations of evolutionists. The ABCs of evolutionism exist nowhere except in the imaginations of evolutionists, their textbooks and the tabloids of the media.

Evolutionary Tabloids.

From time to time, evolutionary tabloids report a new discovery that they believe is destined to rock the scientific world. The colored illustrations depict creatures which are often hysterical nonsense. **(See fig. #8.)** The articles announce that remains of these brutes have been unearthed in an isolated area of the world. The reports say these creatures lived millions of years ago. The writers of these articles beyond belief have only one motive: to sell newspapers and books. The reports are highly exaggerated and full of nonsensical and erroneous statements. There are left only bits of truth because parts of the story have been carefully omitted so that what remains serves their purposes. For example, this amazing report came out of the *Los Angeles Times*:

> Bone Shows Ancestor of Humans Lived Five Million Years Ago
>
> WASHINGTON — "Scientists reported the discovery Wednesday of a five-million-year-old fossil bone fragment of a human-like creature they said is one million years older than the previous oldest known ancestor of mankind. A piece of lower-jaw and two molar teeth ...[1] were all that was found."

Figure #8. TABLOID TALES OF APE-MEN

These incredible fairy tales emerge because evolutionists believe that man has evolved. As a result, they interpret fossil remains to be evidence supporting their theory.

One evolutionist even ventured so far as to trace the origin of the races to the following: The white race came from the chimpanzee, the oriental from the orangutan and the Negro from the gorilla.

Are we humans a freak of Mother Nature? Do we come from a mutant, hairy-bellied, scratching, banana-belching baboon who originated from a glob of primordial slime? Is mankind the product of goo that has come by the way of the zoo, or is he truly a magnificent creature created by an infinitely magnificent Creator? The ABCs of evolutionism are truly a figment of man's imagination. It makes for incredible science fiction.

Chapter Three

The ABCs of Evolutionism

- A - APE-MEN
- B - BATMAN
- C - CATWOMAN
- D - DRYOPITHECUS
- E - ENCINO MAN
- F - FRANKENSTEIN, FRED FLINTSTONE
- G - GIGANTALPITHCUS
- H - HINDU APE-GOD, HOMOHABULUS, HEIDELBERG MAN
- I - ICEMAN
- J - JAVA MAN
- K - KING KONG
- L - LUCY
- M - MISSING LINK
- N - NEBRASKA MAN, NEANDERTHAL MAN, NINJA TURTLES

O - OREOPITHECUS

P - PEKING MAN, PILTDOWN MAN

Q - Q-BERT

R - RAMAPITHECUS

S - SPIDERMAN, SUPERMAN

T - TASADAY STONE AGE TRIBE

U - UNICORN

V - VICTORIAPITHECUS

W - WONDER WOMEN

X - X-MEN

Y - YOSEMITE SAM

Z - ZINJANTHROPUS

Chapter Four

Alien Evolutionism

(See fig. #9.)
Science Fiction in the Laboratory.

Before we investigate these mythological creatures in the ape-men fantasies, it is necessary to point out that some experts in the evolutionary community have escaped to new realms of "reason." Dr. Francis Crick, the famed biologist and Nobel Prize winner for work with the discovery of the DNA molecule (where life begins in the cell), has proposed a "Superman slant." He believes "that life on Earth may have sprung from tiny organisms from a distant planet, sent here by a spaceship as part of a deliberate act of seeding."[2]

ET and Beyond.

These are not the fantasies of just a few eccentric and obscure evolutionists. Dr. Robert Jastrow, celebrated physicist and director of

Figure #9. ALIEN EVOLUTIONISM

NASA's Goddard Institute For Space Studies, asserts that:

> Super-intelligent alien beings will contact us within the next 40 years ... and guide the earth into the galactic community.[2]

These renowned evolutionists don't stop with a passing comment. They are very serious about their fairy-tale-like beliefs. There are scores of books available which go into extensive detail and fantastic speculation on the subject.

Chariots of the Gods.

Chariots of the Gods, a book by Erich von Daniken, is an absurd argument about gods from outer space visiting Earth, bringing a superior form of life previously unknown on Earth. This was effectively discredited by Clifford Wilson in his book *Crash Go the Chariots*.

The popularity of von Daniken's books on extraterrestrial visitors indicates a worldwide desire to find a new, credible theory of evolutionism. Darwin's theory has long been bankrupt of any validity. Von Daniken pointed this out in his book, *According to the Evidence:* "I am afraid that Darwin's theory ... has made generations of paleontologists and anthropologists professionally blind."

Needless to say, von Daniken does not believe in the God of the Bible, and has proposed his own bizarre explanation for man's existence. He believes colonies of creatures existed on other planets and visited Earth to help their "embryonic organisms" develop and mature into the intelligent creature called man.

Carl Sagan's Sad Senseless Space Saga.

Carl Sagan, a well-known professor at Cornell University, produced a 13-part series which aired on national television. It promoted his evolutionary religious fantasy entitled *Cosmos*. I watched the entire series and recorded it for future reference. *Cosmos* settled the question whether evolutionism is a religion. The incredible fantasy begins with the dogmatic statement, "The cosmos is all that is or ever was or ever will be."

Sagan played the part of the "high priest" in the series, which would have been more appropriately dubbed "Sagan's Sad Senseless Space Saga." It proclaimed that man is only composed of "star stuff," has no future and will eventually return to star stuff when he dies. Isn't that a thrilling and glorious future?

Another grand illusion of Sagan's religion is his mythical route to salvation. He believes man's salvation will come from the heavens in the form of extraterrestrials. He is not referring to a supernatural being, but to a physical being from planet in another galaxy. In hopes of confirming his faith, he and others have convinced the United States government to spend enormous amounts of tax dollars to fund his fantasy by sending a series of pictures and music into space aboard one of the space probes. They are hoping that eventually, as the probe drifts beyond our solar system, it will come across another planet inhabited by intelligent beings. Then they will contact earth and have a good influence on earthlings (see page 314 of *Cosmos*). Sagan believes our species and our planet will then be changed forever. In fact, evolutionary space scientists are stepping up their search for intelligent life in the universe. In October 1992, NASA began a program called Project Columbus. Funded by our tax dollars, our government has committed $100 million dollars to the research.

An Extraterrestrial Zookeeper.

Since von Daniken's book, scores of other books have been written by renowned evolutionists discrediting and replacing Darwinism and his view of evolutionism with their own fantastic theories. William D. Hamilton of Oxford University, considered by some to be the most important evolutionary biologist of the second half of this century, writes:

> There's one theory of the universe that I rather like. Suppose our planet is a "zoo for extraterrestrial beings"; they planted the seeds of evolution on earth hoping to create interesting, intelligent creatures. And they watch their experiment, interfering hardly at all. So that almost everything we do comes out according to the laws of nature. But every now and then they see something which doesn't look quite right ... so they insert a finger and just change some little thing."[3]

Such an extraterrestrial-zookeeper deity may not strike everyone as the ideal supreme being. But Hollywood has picked up on the idea and has portrayed this in numerous movies. Here we have the makings of a tale that is stranger than fiction, and more bizarre than those found in the Twilight Zone. This fantasy is nothing more than pagan mythology of the twenty-first century. The evolutionists are continuously adding more hairy hulks to their lineup.

The Reason for Such Foolish Fairy-Tale Notions.

There is a reason why mythology is acceptable among respectable men of science. A theory as ridiculous and unfounded as evolution would not even be considered if it were not that atheistic scientists are bent on negating the idea of a Creator.

In actuality, the issue is and always has been God — the Creator of the universe. The evolutionist desires to be the king and ruler of his life. So it doesn't matter how much evidence there is for creation; it will not make one speck of difference for the individual who refuses to bow his knee to the true Creator. For such a person, God cannot exist.

Respect and Courtesy.

It is inappropriate to poke fun at scientists who have spent years working, studying analyzing to learn more about the world in which we live. Christians should avoid casting scorn upon eminent men of science. My gratification in this book is to attack the king of fools, Satan — the source of such nonsense. He has deceived man into believing this foolishness.

Evolutionists add a generous measure of their own wishful thinking to the evidence. My fun in this volume is to mock the father of lies and the deceiver of men's minds. Satan didn't evolve; he devolved. He is a half-breed of the worst kind — a fallen, condemned, angelic fool. He was once an angel, but was corrupted as a result of his own selfish and rebellious heart. His end will be eternal damnation in the lake of fire (Rev. 20:10).

Chapter Five

The Ape-Man Family Tree

(See fig. #10.)
Visions from Hell.

We all have seen ape-like cavemen illustrated in pictures or in evolutionary films, shuffling along or squatting, with a dull and dim-witted expression. Artists' rendering in the past of what they imagined ancient man looked like have been quite amusing. **(See fig. #11.)** However, in recent evolutionary books many of the images have taken on a much more hideous and repulsive appearance. They could have been inspired only by the unholy spirit of Satan. **(See fig. #12.)** He is out to destroy the biblical account of the first man, Adam, at all cost. Man was created in God's own image — a beauty of perfection hard to envision.

Illustrations of grim looking creatures are depicted and abound in public school textbooks. The explanations given make the reader think those crea-

Figure #10. APE-MAN FAMILY TREE

THE ABCs OF EVOLUTIONISM

Figure #11. AMUSING EVOLUTIONARY APE-MEN

Figure #12. UNHOLY INSPIRATION

tures existed and have been proven to be ancestors of modern man. Nothing could be farther from the truth. Keep in mind Walter Cronkite's statement mentioned in the first chapter:

> Even though we "know" man came from ape, all the bones linking man with ape that have been found in the last 100 years would not even cover a billiard's table.

The Production of the Ape-Man Family Tree (Chart).

The following illustration **(see fig. #13)** shows a typical evolutionary presentation of how man evolved from a small primate to his present form. This chart gives the impression that the creature on the left appeared first. Then from that point on, various forms evolved in a reasonably consistent, consecutive way. Once again, it must be stated that although fossil bones and fragments of skulls and skeletons have been found, the creatures on the chart have never been accurately and positively identified as having existed, let alone evolving one from the other.

Furthermore, the names assigned to these hairy hulks seem to fit the overall features of these freaks of nature — pliopithecus, dryopithecus, oreopithecus, etc. **(See fig. #22.)** These gibberish words sound like a child while eating lunch from a bowl of alphabet soup. Tongue-twister-names add dignity to a pitiful image.

It appears the fruit of the ape-man family tree is suffering from a blight, causing a meager and puny yield. It has yet to produce one promising harvest over the last "several million years."

Filling in the Gaps.

It is hard to believe the ape-man family tree proposed by evolutionists is so sparse. To make matters worse, an examination of the ages assigned by the evolutionists to the clan of "ape-men" reveals that the first five figures in the sequence were contemporaries of one another — they lived in the same time period. The same is true with those at the other end of the time scale. **(See fig. #14)** There is an 11 million year gap in the ape-man family tree between Mr. Ramapithecus and Mr. Australopithecus. In addition, there are also other gaps which amount to hundreds of thousands of years in which no links have yet been found. As we consider the evidence from anthropology (the study of ancient man), it becomes obvious that the term "missing link" is inappropriate. What is missing is the entire chain of ape-man links. In other words, the

Figure #13. A TYPICAL EVOLUTIONARY CHART

The Ape-Man Family Tree

Figure #14. GLARING GAPS OF EVOLUTIONISM

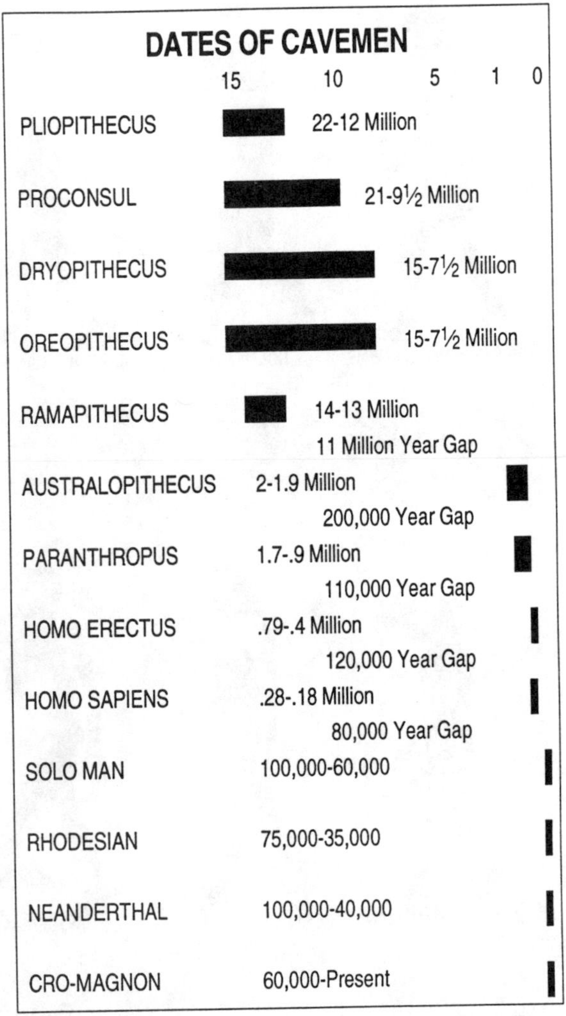

DATES OF CAVEMEN

| | 15 | 10 | 5 | 1 | 0 |

PLIOPITHECUS	22-12 Million
PROCONSUL	21-9½ Million
DRYOPITHECUS	15-7½ Million
OREOPITHECUS	15-7½ Million
RAMAPITHECUS	14-13 Million
	11 Million Year Gap
AUSTRALOPITHECUS	2-1.9 Million
	200,000 Year Gap
PARANTHROPUS	1.7-.9 Million
	110,000 Year Gap
HOMO ERECTUS	.79-.4 Million
	120,000 Year Gap
HOMO SAPIENS	.28-.18 Million
	80,000 Year Gap
SOLO MAN	100,000-60,000
RHODESIAN	75,000-35,000
NEANDERTHAL	100,000-40,000
CRO-MAGNON	60,000-Present

Figure #15. EVOLUTIONARY TREE OF DEATH

ape-man family tree has yet to produce any fruit. **(See fig. #15.)**

The Empty Coffin.

One stubborn fact is that if all the recovered bones of supposedly prehistoric man were brought together, they wouldn't even fill one coffin. **(See fig. #16.)** If man has been around for millions of years, where are all the other bones?

The ape-man charts that evolutionists use in

Figure #16. THE EMPTY COFFIN

their books about evolutionism are nothing more than a figment of their imagination. As we investigate the rest of the story about these so-called "missing links," it will become obvious that the basis for each is a Hollywood fantasy on the level with Batman, Catwoman and Planet of the Apes' trilogies. As we shall see, the ABCs of evolutionism are letters from an illusionary alphabet.

Chapter Six

The Missing Chain

(See fig. #17.)

In one of the books published by *Readers Digest* titled *The Last Two Million Years*, we find a most amazing statement: "In Darwin's time there was little evidence to support his theory, but since then a whole chain of missing links has been established by studying fossil bones." If I understand this correctly, the chain is still missing. In fact, the entire chain has been filled in with missing links. It seems strange that the evolutionists would make this admission, but it couldn't be more truthfully stated. To this day the links are still missing!

Let's Change the Name.

In recent years it has become in vogue to refer to "missing links" as "transitional forms." Lately the buzzword for "missing links" has changed again to the phrase "ancient common

Figure #17. THE LAST OF THE MISSING LINKS

ancestor." In his book, *Evolution in Turmoil*, Dr. Henry Morris points out the reason for the change in terminology:

> Any discussion of specific fossils is out-of-date almost as soon as it is published, so it is almost redundant to critique the hominids currently in vogue. The once-fashionable names of Java Man, Piltdown Man, Nebraska Man, Heidelberg Man, Rhodesia Man, Peking Man and others which used to be offered as proof of man's evolution, are nowadays all but ignored in anthropological discussions. Neanderthal Man and Cro-Magnon Man are universally accepted as homo sapiens today. Even Ramapithecus is now out of favor as an early hominid.

The First "Missing Link."

When the first few "ancient" bones were found in the mid-1800s, evolutionists were anxious to prove their theory. They misinterpreted the few fragments and drew ape-men pictures depicting what man's ancestors supposedly looked like. **(See fig. #18.)**

It is a well-known fact that those original

Figure #18. THE ORIGINAL MISSING LINK

fragments were misrepresented and the caveman pictures were wrong. The 15th edition of the *Encyclopedia Britannica* (1973-74, p. 911) points this out:

> The popular conception that those people were slouched in posture and walked with a shuffling, bent-kneed gait seems to have been due in large part to faulty reconstruction of the skull base and to misinterpretation of certain features of the limb bones of one of the Neanderthal skeletons discovered early in the 20th century.

Did you get that? There was a "misinterpretation ... of one of the Neanderthal skeletons." There were several skeletons from which to choose, so why did they misinterpret them? They selected the one that looked like it might support their theory of ape-man. The zeal of evolutionists has not slackened, and many people still believe that there is plenty of evidence in favor of man descending from the apes. However, we shall see that the evidence today carries the same tune as the first discovery of bones in 1856.

Time Will Tell the Truth.

When we read about new discoveries believed to be the link between man and ape, we can assume that the rest of the story will come forth, in time, revealing similar wrong conclusions made by people who refuse to accept the One and only original Ancestor and Creator of man.

Where Are the "Missing Links?"

If the theory of a slow evolutionary process of producing new creatures from amoeba to man **(see fig. #19)** were true, there would be millions

Figure #19. AMOEBA TO MAN

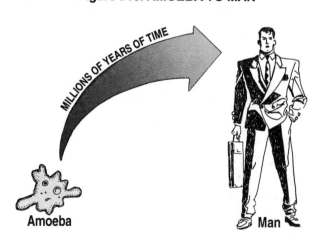

of connecting links all along the way. These intermediate forms should also exist between ape and man. The problem is, not only are there no connecting links between the different kinds of creatures, but there are no connecting links between ape and man. The whole chain is missing, and not one link has been found.

The evolutionists deny this. They insist that ape-man fossils connecting the links have been found. They point to a group of bones they believe represent ancient man. But their belief that these are "missing links" is based on supposition, not fact. Even if the skeletal fragments evolutionists insist belonged to ape-men were "missing links," there still remains an enormous gulf between those supposed ape-men and man.

The Missing Chain (see fig. #20).

Suppose a chain crossed the United States between Los Angeles and New York City — a distance of nearly 3,000 miles. This chain represents the time line of man's three million years of supposed history, each mile representing 1,000 years. Suppose Los Angeles represents mother ape, and New York City represents man. Each city in between represents a link of the chain or an ape-man link in man's history. If only a few cities in between — Denver, St. Louis, Chicago and Pittsburgh — are representing links, then there is much more missing than a few

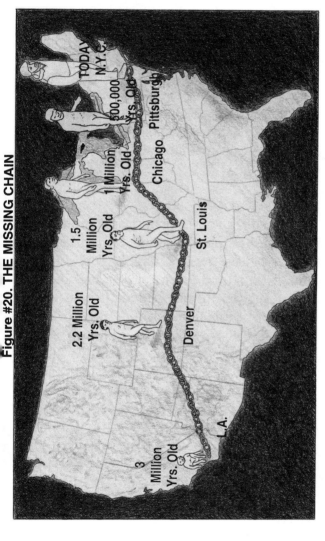

Figure #20. THE MISSING CHAIN

links. There are not enough links even to call it a chain. This is the predicament with the ape-man family tree proposed by evolutionism. It is not links that are missing in the chain; it is the whole chain. This is why the term "missing link" was changed to "transitional form" and then later to "ancient common ancestor." "Missing link" has become an embarrassment to the evolutionary community.

All in the Family.

It should be noted that the reason evolutionists now use the phrase "ancient common ancestor" rather than "missing link" or "transitional form" is to release them from the pressure of recognizing our original ancestor. Instead, each skull found is said to be a part of man's overall family. They no longer attempt to place the skull into the missing chain.

Evolutionists today study and assign significance to each skull independently. They have changed the rules of the game so that they no longer have to be responsible to try to make the pieces of their puzzle fit. Every skull is considered part of the family — no matter how distant a relative it is! And, of course, if they run into any problems, they can just change the rules again.

In *Ape-Man, the Story of Human Evolution*, a recent book by Rod Caird, the author suggests that man's origins will never be discovered because the definition of man is so subjective. According to evolutionism, there is no God. So evolutionists do not believe His Word or in its absolute truth. They believe man must determine his own meaning and purpose for existence. This leaves the door wide open for abortion, euthanasia or infanticide, as well as freedom to study man's origins without pressure to find the "missing link."

In the following chapters we shall take a closer look at the "proofs" of "missing links." We shall see that they are still missing and that the artists' conceptions that have personified the fragments are purely science fiction. We will see that each of the ABCs of evolutionism is produced from a mythological alphabet, which is traveling on an imaginary road to nowhere.

Chapter Seven

Extinct Ape-Men Charts: (The Road to Fantasyland)

Dusty Ol' Charts.

In spite of the fact that the so-called "evidences" are just meager bits and pieces **(See fig. #21.)** evolutionists continue their relentless search for the missing links that exist only in their imaginations. They find it necessary to constantly revise their charts tracing the route by which apes mutated into humans. The charts become outdated about as fast as they come into existence. These charts are short-lived because the pieces of the puzzle will not cooperate with the ideas and imaginations of the evolutionists. For example, *National Geographic*, (11/85) has an ape-man chart which depicts a number of nonexistent creatures which have become "extinct" within the last ten years. Let's take a look at some of the original cast members of the

Figure #21. THE MEAGER EVIDENCE

	Skulls	Jaws	Teeth	Pelvis	Femurs	Vertebre	Arm & Hand	Legs & Foot	Palate	Ribs
Pliopithecus	1			1		2				
Proconsul		2	6				4	2		
Dryopithecus			4		1		2	1		
Oreopithecus	Frag.			1	1		1	2		1
Ramapithecus		2	3						1	
Australopithecus	3		2	1		2		2		
Paranthropus	2	2	4					2		
Homo Erectus	1		5					1		
Homo Sapiens	3									
Solo Man	Frag.							2		
Rhodesian	1	1							1	
Neanderthal	16	45	200+	26	23	600+	41	34	Whole Skel.	
Cro-Magnon	Blends into Modern Man — Many Skeletons									

so-called transitional forms who are no longer part of the team, as seen in *Time Life Nature* book, *Early Man*. **(See fig. #13.)**

Dryopithecus. (see fig. #22)

The letter "D" of the evolutionary alphabet stands for Dryopithecus. The ape chart begins on the left. Here we have an ape named Dryopithecus with no human characteristics. When his bones were unearthed, he was thought to be a link between ape and man. Today he is considered to be nothing more than a member of the ape family.

Gigantolpithecus (see fig. #22).

The letter "G" stands for the next fellow on the chart with the distinguished name of Mr. Gigantolpithecus. At one time, he was considered to be a missing link, but today evolutionists believe his remains are nothing more than those of an extinct giant ape. In *Time* magazine (11/7/77), Richard Leakey, one of the world's most recognized anthropologists, removed this creature from the ape-to-man chart.

Ramapithecus: Hindu Ape-God (see fig. #23).

Cross a Hindu god with an ape and what do

Extinct Ape-Men Charts:
(The Road to Fantasyland)

Figure #22. RETIREES FROM THE ORIGINAL CAST

GIGANTOPITHECUS

OREOPITHECUS

DRYOPITHECUS

Figure #23. THE HINDU APE-GOD

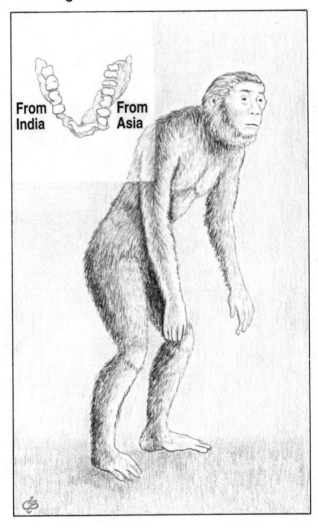

Extinct Ape-Men Charts:
(The Road to Fantasyland)

you get? You get a Hindu ape-god which represents letter "H" of the evolutionary ape-man alphabet. Given the dignified name of Ramapithecus (Rama is a Hindu god and Pithecus means ape), this mythological creature was believed to be another missing link, an ape-man, an ancestor of man. Based on a two-inch fragment of a skull and a few teeth found some 60 years ago in India and a piece of jaw found later in Africa, the creature must have had a split personality! The "experts" put the fragments together and out came Ramapithecus, an ape-man that walked upright like humans, but of course had a little hunch in its back.

Artists' renditions of Ramapithecus include his height, length of arms, head shape — and even the kind of beard he had. With such details, one would think the artists had a complete skeleton along with its portrait, ID and diary from which to work. However, all that was found was a jawbone and some teeth. The reason the principle researchers thought this creature should be added to the lineage of ape-to-man was because its jaw structure was closer to man than the ape. It is interesting to note that this same tooth and jaw structure is found in baboons that live in Ethiopia today. Baboons are not in the lineage of man. They are not part ape and part man, but fully ape.

Well, the dream ended like a nightmare. Since the time the original fossils were found, more complete skeletons have been discovered of this same creature. Ramapithecus has been found to be nearly identical to the modern orangutan apes.[4] **(See fig. #24.)**

Today, the principle researcher, David Pilbeam thinks that Ramapithecus belongs to a third lineage that has no relationship to the modern ape or man. The same men who originally put this ape-man in the chart have now removed it.

Exceptions or the Rule?

One might suggest that we have picked a few exceptions and not the rule. However, this is not the case. In fact, according to the evolutionary ape-man chart, there is not a single form with a complete skeleton to support its existence — until Neanderthal Man, (covered in Part III) which now has been fully accepted by the evolutionary community to be 100% human.

This lack of evidence clearly reveals the illusory nature of the evolutionists' claim that the evolution of man has been proven. We do not have room in this book to cover all the ape-man alphabet, so we shall select several fantasy apemen from the ape-man alphabet and discuss them in detail in the following chapters.

Extinct Ape-Men Charts:
(The Road to Fantasyland)

Figure #24. THE REAL RAMAPITHECUS

PART II
FOUR FUNERALS FOR FOUR EVOLUTIONARY FANTASIES
(The Rest of the Stories)

Chapter 8: The Ape-Man Syndrome

Chapter 9: Funeral One: In Memory of Java Man (1891-1921)
Pithecanthropus Erectus

Chapter 10: Funeral Two: In Memory of Nebraska Man (1925-1927)
Hesperopithecus

Chapter 11: Funeral Three: In Memory of Nellie (1927-1940)
Peking Man

Chapter 12: Funeral Four: In Memory of Piltdown Man (1912-1953)
Eoanthropus Dawsoni

Chapter Eight

The Ape-Man Syndrome

Filling in the Missing Lines.

Remember the fun activity magazines designed to keep children busy and quiet? The pictures had to be completed by filling in the missing lines. Beginning with number one, the missing lines were filled in between the numbers. Once the lines were completed, one could see the picture of a person, animal or some other object.

It seems like evolutionists have enjoyed this same diversion. However, every time they fill in the missing lines, or "links," their creatures look the same. It is known as the ape-man syndrome. It doesn't matter if there are 10, 100 or 1000 numbers, the creature always looks half-ape and half-human. **(See fig. #25.)**

Instead of numbers, evolutionists use bone fragments. They may have a pig's tooth, an elephant's kneecap, an ape's jawbone or a donkey's

The Ape-Man Syndrome

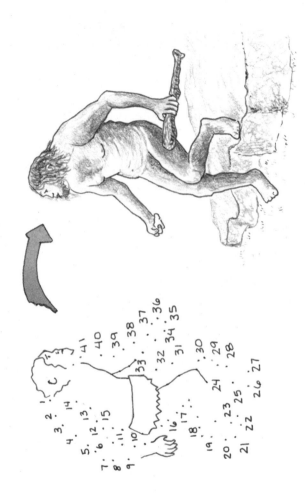

Figure #25. THE APE-MAN SYNDROME

Figure #26. THE MISSING LINK — ALWAYS LOOKS THE SAME

HEY MAN, WE'VE GOT OUR RIGHTS TOO.

skull cap, but when they have finished, the reconstruction inevitably looks like a "missing link" — a cross between a big-footed buffoon and a banana-belching baboon. **(See fig. #26.)**

This newspaper article from the Associated Press titled, *Remote Ancestor of Man Believed*

Found in Nepal is an example:

> KATMANDU, Nepal (AP) — A joint U.S.-Nepal scientific expedition has found evidence of "possible human ancestors" in the rocks of the Himalayan foothills, an American scientist with the researchers reports. "We have found a tooth" ... said Dr. Jens Munthe of Milwaukee, Wisconsin, co-leader of the expedition.

Since evolutionists believe that men came from apes, they must imagine these "ape-men" into existence. One scientist admitted:

> Bones say nothing about the fleshy parts of the nose, lips or ears. Artists must create something between an ape and a human being; the older the specimen is said to be, the more ape-like they make it.[5]

The Truth Comes Out.

Ronald Ervin has worked as senior medical illustrator at the University of Iowa and as a medical art consultant at the University of Virginia. He has drawn medical and scientific illustrations for textbooks, journals and even for courtrooms. When Ervin was called upon to recreate australopithecus like the famous "Lucy" for a book, he was told to make her more apelike in appearance because the author thought his original illustrations were too human-like.

Since the remains of Lucy didn't contain much of the skull, Ron had simply attempted to keep his drawing within the context of the normal anatomy of the rest of the bones, which he was using for reference. Nevertheless, he was asked to alter his picture of Lucy to conform with the evolutionary transitional creatures as the biology's evolutionary textbook's author requested.

Artists' Reconstruction.

It is crucial when considering the truth of fossil reconstruction to ask what evidence was used to produce such a picture. Sometimes the evidence is extremely scanty. Bias often enters into the picture, and drawings are based more on preconceived ideas than on actual evidence. Keep in mind these are the facts for an evolutionary reconstruction of an ape-man.
1. Often only fragments are the evidence.
2. Ape bones are fashioned to look human.
3. Human bones are fashioned to look apelike.

The Ape-Man Syndrome

4. It is impossible to tell what the hair, nose, eyes, lips and ears looked like from the skull, so they are added according to the direction and instruction of the evolutionist. **(See fig. #27A and #27B)**

Books and magazines confidently illustrate ape-men as stooped over and hairy, but the evidence is extremely flimsy and there is a great amount of imaginative speculation. Many a "fossil man" is based on fragments of a skull or jawbone, a few teeth, or maybe a leg bone. **(See fig. #28.)** There are plenty of fossils of apes and humans. Where are the multitudes of in-between links? Their absence speaks volumes.

Imaginary Ape-Man.

A typical example of the unique imagination of the evolutionist is the reconstruction of the skull Afarensis, a key fossil-link of evolutionism. Only the light-colored bones and teeth were actually found. The dark-colored bone is pure imagination. **(See fig. #29.)**

It is easy to recognize evolutionism is a 21st-century fantasy when it becomes obvious that so much of such an important evolutionary fossil is a product of imagination — not to mention the fact that the skull cap and the facial bones may not even come from the same skeleton!

Figure #27A. HOW TO FABRICATE AN APE-MAN
EVOLUTIONARY STEPS IN RECONSTRUCTING A FOSSIL HEAD

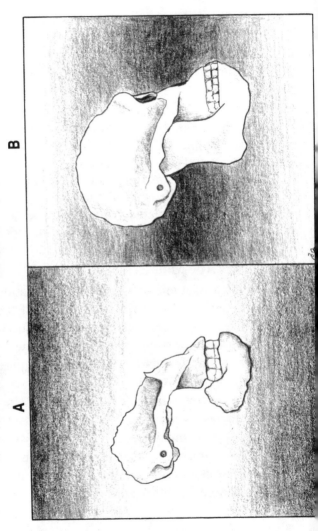

The Ape-Man Syndrome

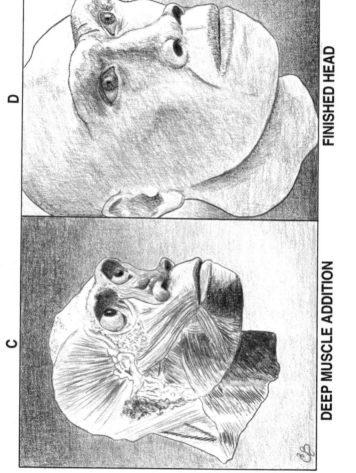

C — DEEP MUSCLE ADDITION

D — FINISHED HEAD

Figure #28. BEFORE AND AFTER

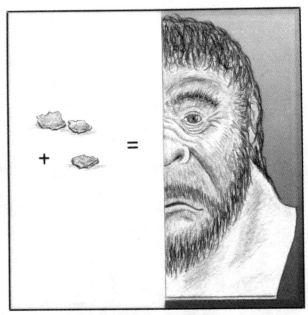

BEFORE & AFTER

Orce Man.

Another supposed human ancestor was recently discovered in Spain. It was declared by Spanish evolutionary "experts" to be the skull cap of the oldest fossil man ever discovered in Europe. The nearby village where it was found, Orce, had the distinguished privilege of being used to name this "ancient human." However, it wasn't long before the experts in France revealed that the skull cap was actually that of a six-month old donkey.[6]

No "missing link" has ever been found! Each one has been proven to be something else, usually an ape or occasionally a human. But no fossil

Figure #29. FILLING IN WITH AN IMAGINARY MIND

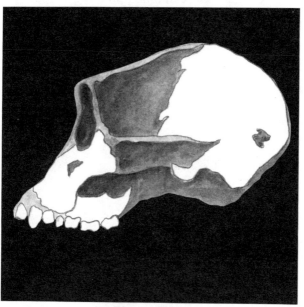

❑ Plaster Fill in
■ Original Pieces

has ever been found that was something in between.

Just as the lines in evolutionary funded magazines (such as *National Geographic* and *Science Digest*) always end up as ape-men, so it is with the alphabet of evolutionism. Each letter always turns up as a half-breed, half-ape and half-man.

We shall now examine four alleged ape-men and share the rest of their stories, which truly reveal the reality of the ape-man syndrome. Evolution is truly nothing more than a cult involving monkey mythology, the ultimate aim of which is to worship man as lord and king of the universe.

Chapter Nine

Funeral One: In Memory of Java Man (1891-1921) Pithecanthropus Erectus

(See fig. #30.)
The Ascension of Java Man.

Pithecanthropus Erectus, better known as Java Man, was discovered by Dr. Dubois. *Pithe* refers to apes, and *anthropus* means man. *Erectus* refers to the erect posture. Immediate reconstructions of Mr. Java's remains included all the hairs on his head.

The sculptor fashioned Java Man with his forehead sharply receding and added a heavy-brow ridge above the deep-set eyes. The head was thrust forward on the shoulders, with a jutting mouth, half-open, showing apelike teeth. This is interesting, since all that was found was a piece of a skull cap, a femur and a thigh bone. **(See fig. #31.)** A worried expression was added to the face along with an apelike gaze, no doubt to suggest a limited mental capacity. Clearly, the facial characteristics of Java Man are pure imagination.

Figure #30. JAVA MAN

Funeral One: In Memory of Java Man (1891-1921)
Pithecanthropus Erectus

Figure #31. THE MISSING PIECES

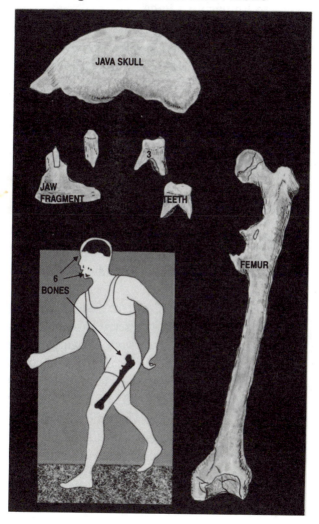

How to Fabricate a Face.

Neither hair, skin nor flesh was found, so the artist followed instructions provided by the evolutionary community to fashion these ingredients. Fossil bones give no indication whatsoever of Mr. Java, or for that matter any deceased person or creature, being hairy or hairless, light or dark skinned, or any facial expression. Since the lower part of the back of the skull was not found, it cannot be known whether or not the head was thrust forward on the shoulders. Since only three teeth and a fragment of the jaw were unearthed, the nose could have been flat and apelike as portrayed, or it could have been magnificent like that of Jimmy Durante, W.C. Fields or Charles de Gaulle.

Since the shape and size of the nose and ears and the amount of hair are not preserved in fossils, they are all reconstructed by guesswork. Imagine what an evolutionist would create for the nose of a proboscis monkey if he were extinct and the first fossil remains were found today. **(See fig. #32.)** Since it is totally flesh, there is no way of knowing unless the monkey left his picture ID beside him. Even though nearly all of Mr. Java was missing, plaster casts of his supposed image were placed in museums, and his photographs appeared in textbooks and encyclopedias all over the world.

Figure #32. A PRONOUNCED PROBOSCIS POSSESSION

Figure #33. WHERE IN THE WORLD IS JAVA?

The Rest of the Story.

Found in Java in 1891 **(see fig. #33)**, Mr. Java was claimed to have lived 500,000 years ago. Smithsonian Institute's report of 1913[7] reveals the following:

In 1891, a man named Dubois discovered a molar tooth while digging for fossils in a river in Java. The following month, he found the top part of a skull about three feet away from where he had found the tooth. (Question: If the skull cap was found only three feet away from the tooth, why did it take a month to discover it?) A year later, he found a thigh bone about fifty feet from where he found the tooth and skull top. One month later, he found another molar tooth. These four bones were found in a region where the remains of many animal bones lay. The bones were found between 1891 and 1899. A third tooth was found about two miles away and was reported as belonging to the same type of hominid. All these findings were put together and Java Man appeared.

After a brief public showing, Dubois locked up the remains of Mr. Java, keeping any further scientific inquiry from taking place for the next 30 years. All of what was known about Java Man came from what the finder, Dubois, disclosed. No one knew whether or not he told the truth about the remains. Finally, after 30 years, pressure from the scientific community forced Dubois to hand over his finds for critical examination. I don't have to tell you what the conclusions were. Java Man died at the ripe young age of 30.

Enchanted with the theory of evolutionism, Dubois had gone to Java as a young doctor. He told his friends that he was going to bring back the "missing-link."[8]

It wasn't until 30 years later that DuBois reported the skull cap of Java Man was that of a gibbon. He also admitted he found human skulls 15-20 feet away, but kept them hidden because, he claims, he didn't fully understand their significance.

Meanwhile, the ghost of Mr. Java is still at large, as he is still presented in many textbooks as one of our long-lost ancestors in a long line of evolutionary fantasies. **(See fig. #34.)**

Java Man II.

There is an even more remarkable sequel to the evolutionary illusion — Pithy II found in Java in 1926. However, this amazing discovery believed at first to be evidence for the "missing link," turned out to be the knee bone of an extinct elephant![9]

Figure #34. THE PASSING OF JAVA MAN

Chapter Ten

Funeral Two: In Memory of Nebraska Man (1925-1927) Hesperopithecus

(See fig. #35.)
Scopes' Monkey Trial.

In 1925 a trial took place in Dayton, Tennessee, that received worldwide publicity. It was misrepresented to the world as a trial between evolutionism and biblical creationism. There was a confrontation between two famous lawyers, William Jennings Bryan, a Christian, and Clarence Darrow, a skeptic. Mr. Darrow, an agnostic, interrogated Mr. Bryan on the witness stand regarding trivial questions about the Bible and his personal beliefs. Darrow made Bryan appear foolish and ignorant. As a result, the media focused on this aspect of the trial and spread to the world the image that Christians who believe in biblical creation were ignorant fundamentalists.

Figure #35. NEBRASKA MAN

The actual purpose of the trial was and still is overlooked even today when references to it are made by evolutionists. The purpose of the trial was simply to determine if public school teacher John Scopes could continue to teach evolutionism, since the law in Tennessee at that time allowed only the biblical account of creation to be taught.

Today, the situation has reversed. These same constitutional questions are being raised because only one view is permitted to be taught in the public schools — evolutionism.

Scopes' Pig Trial.

At the Scopes' trial, the evidence in favor of evolutionism was the remains of what was believed to be a "missing link" between man and his ancestor ape, Hesperopithecus, better known as Mr. Nebraska. What were the remains of Mr. Nebraska? A tooth! **(See fig. #36.)** From the tooth, an artist drew a race of people and claimed they lived one million years ago. Earlier, there was a "replica" of Nebraska Man in the museum at the University of Nebraska. In fact, it may still be there.

A Cornhusker Whale of a Tale.

Someone found a tooth in Nebraska, home of the Cornhuskers, and sent it to evolutionary scientists in the East. The scientists examined the tooth and introduced "Nebraska Man" to the

Figure #36. THE CUSP OF HESPEROPITHECUS

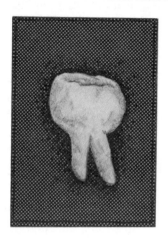

world. Henry Fairfield Osborn — a professor at Columbia University, an eminent paleontologist of that day — as well as several other authorities, proclaimed to the public, "Here we have proof of what early man was like in North America." Osborn declared:

> The earth spoke to Bryan (the Christian lawyer in the Scopes' trial), from his own state of Nebraska. The Hesperopithecus tooth is like the still, small voice; its sound is by no means easy to hear. This little tooth speaks volumes of truth, in that it affords evidence of man's descent from the ape.

This one little tooth was their "proof" of what early man was like in North America. The London *Daily Illustrated News* displayed a full-page spread on Nebraska Man. The scientific name given to this prestigious find was HESPEROPITHECUS HAROLD COOK II (meaning Harold Cook's ape of the west). The newspaper also portrayed Mr. Nebraska Man's wife.

After the trial, someone suggested returning to the site where the tooth had been found. At the site, the entire jawbone was found and the tooth fit perfectly. Suddenly, the enthusiasm of the scientists turned to dismay as they realized they had made a grave mistake: The jaw was from an extinct pig!

Let's Make-Believe.

It is amazing that Nebraska Man was dignified by the scientific name, Hesperopithecus Harold Cook II, from only a tooth. The evolutionists were so desperate to find an ape-man that they allowed their imaginations to run wild over a tooth. They put it into a make-believe skull, then put the skull onto a make-believe skeleton. The make-believe skeleton was covered with make-believe flesh and a furry coat and given a make-believe wife. **(See fig. #37.)** Figure #37

Figure #37. FAMILY PORTRAIT

was taken from a London newspaper which was published during the year of the Scopes' trial.

Two years after the Scopes' trial, Nebraska Man returned to being just a pig's tooth. Another tooth just like it was found. This time the tooth was attached to its owner's skull. The skull was attached to the entire skeleton. The remains turned out to be another member of the same species of extinct pigs.

The leading scientific authorities who had ridiculed Mr. Bryan at the trial for his supposed ignorance had created an entire human race out of a single tooth that came from a pig! What an embarrassment to the evolutionary community. Of course, there was little publicity about the discovery of this error. It seems that no one wants to end up looking like a monkey. This is how the testimony of "experts" is often used to manipulate and intimidate Christians.

Another Toothless Brainstorm.

The evolutionary community has gone to great lengths to try to bridge the gap between man and monkey. There was another feeble attempt made again: The reconstruction was based upon only one tooth. This particular tooth was not found in the ground, but was purchased in a drugstore in Hong Kong. Evolutionists used this one tooth and a great deal of imagination to furnish the details of muscle structure, ears, nose, fingers and toes for this creature. After reconstructing this "missing link" from one tooth, they discovered it was a molar from a giant wart hog.[10]

The Foul's Tooth.

The pig's tooth used as evidence at the Scopes' trial is now at the Creation Museum just outside the small town of Glen Rose, Texas. Evolutionists tried to make a monkey out of a pig, but the pig ended up making a monkey out of the evolutionists. **(See fig. #38.)**

The Creation Museum, directed by Dr. Carl Baugh, has enough evidence within its small quarters to completely topple the towering myth of evolutionism. The museum is located near Dinosaur State Park in the heart of Texas. For more information, call or write:

Creation Evidences Museum,
Box 309
Glen Rose, TX. 76043
(817) 897-3200

Figure #38. THE PASSING OF NEBRASKA MAN

Chapter Eleven

Funeral Three: In Memory of Nellie (1927-1940) Peking Man

(See fig. #39.)
The Missing Duck.

Some years ago while visiting Peking, China, the members of our tour group attended a banquet hosted by our Chinese guide. The entrée was the internationally known Peking Duck. When the platter arrived, there was plenty of bumpy duck skin but no meat. We carefully searched through the platters for the missing duck, but to no avail. It was a case involving "fowl" play. The tale of Peking Man follows suit.

The evolutionists' Peking Man fits into the category of the elusive "bigfoot" — a half-man and half-ape character. Just as there have been many sightings of bigfoot who supposedly roams the northwestern U.S., there have been a number of eyewitnesses who make some extraordinary claims about Peking Man.

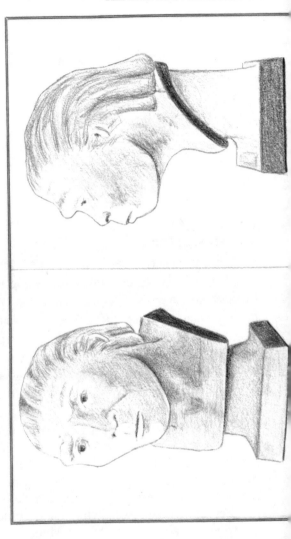

Figure #39. PEKING MAN

The Missing Ape-Man.

When asked for evidence (clear pictures, films, etc.) of Bigfoot, only excuses are given. Likewise, when asked to present the fossil evidence for a closer examination of Peking Man, the evolutionists' answer is, "Well, he's not available for interviews." It seems all the evidence vanished during World War II and hasn't been seen since. Once again, it sounds like there was foul play.

The Rest of the Story.

Peking Man was discovered by Franz Weidenreich in 1927 in a cave near Peking, China among 15 pieces of skulls, and other bones. Using fragments of skulls, they reconstructed a skull and gave it the name, "Nellie." No complete skull could be found. **(See fig. #40.)** As usual, the reconstruction depended on considerable artistic ingenuity. Nellie's skull was badly broken and incomplete. In fact, the lower jaw (without teeth) was actually found about 80 feet higher than the fragments of the skull. There is reason to believe that Nellie is actually a combination of parts from three different creatures. But no one will ever know because Nellie, too, mysteriously disappeared during World War II, so she isn't available for comments. However,

Figure #40. PEKING PUZZLE

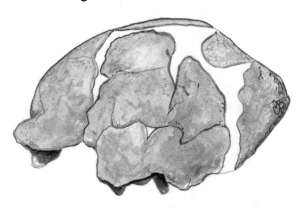

she has numerous supporters who will speak in her behalf and will vouch for her authenticity. As you may suspect, they are all evolutionists, whose evidence is nothing more than a plaster of paris model of the supposed original.

Peking Stew.

That is not the end of the story. In the same cave, remains from a fire, quartz and bones were also found. At some point in ancient history, hunters cooked their prey (sometimes members of the monkey family) in the cave. Remains of several types of animals were found together. Dr. Malcolm Bowden discussed the evidence in his outstanding book, *Ape-man Fact or Fallacy*? Dr. Bowden concluded that Nellie was a type of extinct ape. The broken-up bone fragments were the remains of animals caught, cooked and eaten. The mixture of bones may have been Peking stew or some other type of monkey soup.

Alas, poor Nellie too has fallen by the wayside. As Gary Parker points out in his book, *Creation, The Facts of Life*: "Peking Man seems to have been man's meal, not man's ancestor."

Please Come Home, Nellie.

It is astounding that this missing "ape-man/woman" is still used as evidence of the "missing link." In 1994, a feature four-part documentary series on Ape-man hosted by Walter Cronkite heralded Peking Man as evidence of evolutionism. The film series was accompanied by a beautiful full-color hardbound book, *Apeman the Story of Human Evolution* by Rod Cairn. The book shows Nellie's skull amidst the array of supposed hard-core proofs. Of course, neither the films nor the book mention the mysterious disappearance of Peking Man's remains or that the skull pictured was only a plaster of paris model. This is to be expected since evolutionism has nothing to do with reality, only the figment of evolutionists' wild imaginations — wishful thinking.

Heart Problem.

Men of science long to prove their mental virility by producing "offspring" — a theory that will explain the origin of the universe. Their inability to produce "offspring" is not a problem of genetics; it is a problem of the heart. Having refused to accept the truth that God is the Creator, they have had to invent a lie. That lie is now making monkeys of them. **(See fig. #41.)**

Figure #41. THE PASSING OF PEKING MAN

Chapter Twelve

Funeral Four: In Memory of Piltdown Man (1912-1953) Eoanthropus Dawsoni

(See fig. #42.)
From the Pit to the Palace.

Mr. Piltdown Man was found down in a pit in England. It wasn't long before he was bathed, shaven and elevated to British nobility. Discovered by Charles Dawson, Piltdown Man was announced to the world in 1912 as the "missing link." Arthur Woodward, the director of the Natural History Museum of London, publicly declared this as a monumental discovery. Piltdown Man quickly rose to the top of the evolutionary ape-man chart. He was dignified by the evolutionary community with the formal name Eoanthropus Dawsoni or "Dawn-Man-of-Dawson."

Figure #42. PILTDOWN MAN

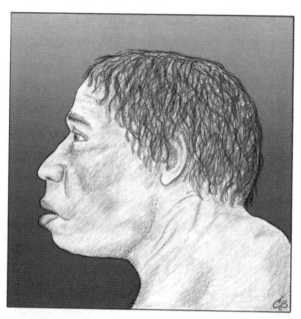

The press was introduced to Mr. Piltdown Man; cameras flashed and photos of Mr. Piltdown's sculptured ape-like bust were released to the public. He became a star overnight and remained a celebrity for the next 40 years.

The remains from which Piltdown Man was reconstructed consisted of a man-like skull cap and an ape-like jawbone. **(See fig. #43.)** He was proclaimed to be 500,000 years old. The scientific community was convinced. For almost a half century, this pitiful fellow was heralded throughout the world by leading evolutionary scientists as the greatest proof for evolutionism. Casts and drawings of him were placed in many museums around the world. Charles Dawson had the dubious honor of having found Mr. Piltdown's remains — dubious because the honor has turned into a dishonorable discharge.

Figure #43. PILTDOWN PUZZLE

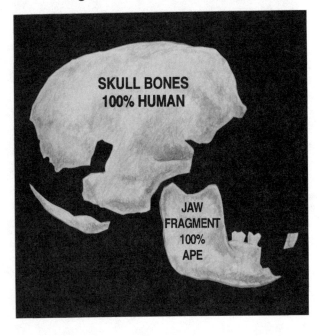

The Rest of the Story.

In 1908, Dawson was sent a fragment of a skull from a gravel pit. Some time later, from the same gravel pit, Dawson obtained two more small parts of a skull. A year later, a jawbone was discovered. The following year, a priest named Teilhard found a tooth. The same gravel pit produced bones of elephants, hippopotamuses, beavers, horses and deer. Fragments from among the remains of all these creatures were selected to put together Piltdown Man.

A skull was molded from plaster of Paris. The creature was fashioned to appear half-ape and half-man. Then the skull fragments were pressed into the plaster cast as they *imagined* them to fit. The rest of the face was fashioned to look like an ape-man. **(See fig. #44.)**

Soon a prominent evolutionist, Sir Arthur Keith, the head of the English Royal College of Surgeons, took issue with Dawson. He claimed that the plaster skull model was too small. He argued that the skull capacity should be about 1,500 cc. instead of the 1,070 cc. **(See fig. #45.)** The battle raged for months and was reported in the magazine *Nature*. Four years after the original skull fragment was found, another tooth was discovered in the gravel pit and was assigned to a place in the upper left jaw. Others were assigned to the lower right jaw.

Figure #44. FILLING IN THE IMAGINARY LINES

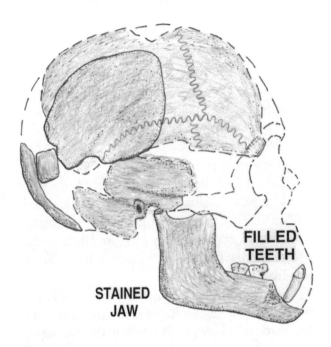

Dental Records Reveal Truth.

It wasn't until 1953 that scientists finally made a critical analysis of Piltdown Man. They discovered the teeth had been filed to appear man-like and the skull had been stained with bichromate of potash so that it would appear old. **(See fig. #46.)** The whole thing was a FRAUD!

Figure #45. WILL THE REAL PILTDOWN SKULL PLEASE EMERGE?

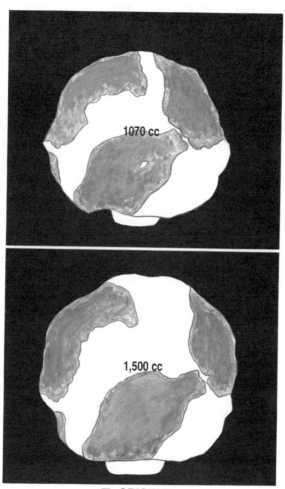

A critical investigation of the jawbone revealed that it had belonged to an ape that had died only 50 years previously. Once again, though this "missing link" had been reconstructed with deception it had completely fooled all the

Figure #46. THE IMPLEMENTS OF CRIME

"experts," who had promoted Mr. Piltdown with the utmost confidence.

How Could Anyone Believe Such a Phony?

Piltdown Man was resurrected again in 1979 to investigate who perpetrated the hoax. However, the real mystery is not who did it, but how could anyone believe it since it wasn't even a clever hoax? The prominent evolutionist Gould even pointed out:

> The evidences of artificial abrasion (filing) immediately sprang to the eye. Indeed so obvious did they seem, it may well be asked — how was it that they had escaped notice before?[11]

200 Doctoral Theses.

For nearly 50 years, Mr. Piltdown was considered one of man's ancestors by the evolutionary community. The *Encyclopedia Britannica* listed Piltdown Man as one of the most important finds of anthropological remains in the world. It has been estimated that at one time there were over 300 replicas of him in various museums worldwide. About 500 books and pamphlets were written in support of this fantasy.

How is it possible that more than 200 doctoral theses were written on Piltdown Man when he was simply a crudely doctored up chimpanzee's jaw attached to a modern human skull? How is it possible that for many decades this hoax dominated textbooks as the chief evidence for man's evolution? Was it because of a small mistake in man's search towards truth? I believe it is because of the strong bias and prejudice of the basic belief system of evolutionism and their continuous rejection of the Creator and His Word. Such bias causes blindness to even the most simple realities.

Last-Ditch Efforts.

In the recently produced four-part video series *Ape-man*, host Walter Cronkite and his colleagues attempted to cover evolutionism's 40-year blunder regarding Piltdown Man by suggesting that the hoax was the result of one of the following scenarios:

1. Scientists in the heart of the British establishment were in on the hoax and knew all about it.
2. England wanted some remains of early man because they didn't have any.
3. Evolutionists knew that eventually they would find the evidence for the "missing link." They just wanted to help by manufacturing something that they believed would be found sooner or later anyway.
4. Since the above three excuses were so ridiculous, evolutionists came up with a fourth excuse. They have attempted to cover their blunder by searching for a

witness who lived at the time of the hoax and who did not agree with the original conclusions. They found one: In 1914, the American Museum of Natural History published an article by famous American paleontologist, William King Gregory, entitled, *The Dawn Man of Piltdown, England*. A portion of the article which opposed Piltdown Man was read on the video.

> It has been suspected by some that geologically they are not old at all, that they may represent a deliberate hoax, a Negro or Australian skull and a broken ape-jaw artificially fossilized and planted in the gravel-bed to fool the scientists.[12]

Nothing New.

There were of course, those who wouldn't accept the Piltdown Man. There are always some who won't accept a colleague's pet theories. And there were evolutionists who did not agree with the conclusions some made regarding Piltdown Man. But the truth is, the evolutionary world at large *was* fooled. Did you notice the reference to the Negro or Australian skull by Mr. Gregory?

Why did he suggest a Negro or Australian skull was used? The Australian aboriginal and the Negro were considered to be on the level of a gorilla. Anyone who has studied the works of the early evolutionists will see the glaring racist statements throughout their literature. Walter Cronkite intentionally overlooked this in his video because the average person would never have caught it unless they were well-informed on the history of evolutionism.

Open Season On Aborigines.

At one time it was believed that aborigines were less evolved, so they were not treated like humans. Evolutionists in the late 1800s paid 10 shillings for skulls of aborigines that were in good condition. They used them in research in conjunction with the British Museum. The skulls were also sought after by evolutionists in Germany for their museums.[13] The issue of racism and how evolutionism promotes it will be covered in Parts IX and X.

Lessons Learned.

We can learn a valuable lesson here. Those in the scientific world have the same problem people have everywhere in the world: ego. Ego drives men to do things in hopes of becoming famous. The origin of man is what they want to prove, and they don't seem to care whether their "evidence" is genuine or not. If creation scientists were guilty of such an approach, they would be widely denounced.

When people want to believe strongly in evolutionism, they see only what they want to see. In short, evolutionary believers have decided their theory is true, and will subscribe to *anything* that will support their theory. In the case of Piltdown Man and others, evolutionists thought they had found the evidence for which they were looking. In their excitement, even the most respected researchers overlooked obvious file-marks on the teeth and the stains on the skull. Mr. Piltdown fooled the world's greatest experts. Once a person rejects the Word of God, he opens himself up to deception. On the other hand, those who trust the Word of God will be protected by the hand of God.

Piltdown Man has finally been removed from his palatial pedestal and buried in a pit near where he was found. There is even a headstone for visitors who would like to come and render their last respects! Poor 'ol Piltdown, he was once thought to be a gem, but turned out to be an inhumane joke. **(See fig. #47.)**

Figure #47. THE PASSING OF PILTDOWN MAN

PART III
THE NEANDERTHAL RACE

- **Chapter 13**: The Emergence of Ape-Man
- **Chapter 14:** Mr. Neanderthal (1856)
- **Chapter 15:** The Elephant Man
- **Chapter 16:** Neanderthal's Relatives
- **Chapter 17:** A Face-Lift for the Neaderthals and a Change of Face for the Evolutionists
- **Chapter 18:** The Iceman of the Ice Age
- **Chapter 19:** Variety Within the Human Species

Chapter Thirteen

The Emergence of Ape-Man

The Rise of Ape-Man.

The idea of evolutionism didn't begin with Darwin. Many scientists believed it before his day. In fact, it was believed and taught among the Greeks. Long before the birth of Christ, the idea existed that men evolved from fish, and that animals had come from plants, and that insects and flies suddenly appeared from mud. These theories were just as unbiblical and unscientific then as the present-day theory of evolutionism is. The reason people concoct such theories is to discredit the idea of God as the Creator. People believed in the theory back then for the same reason they believe in evolutionism today. In fact, evolutionism is nothing more than an elaborate sophisticated philosophical version of the old superstition that life suddenly appeared out of mud.

By the time Charles Darwin became famous

in the middle of the 1800s after publishing his book *The Origins of the Species*, the evolutionary community was busy searching for any link to confirm their religion of evolutionism. It wasn't long before the idea of the first ape-man emerged. Meet Mr. Neanderthal.

Chapter Fourteen

Mr. Neanderthal (1856)

(See fig. #48.)
The Emergence of Neanderthal.

Homo Neanderthalensis' (or the Neanderthal Man's) remains were first discovered in a cave in western Germany in 1856. Neanderthal is the name for the valley in Germany where skeletal remains have been found. At one time evolutionary anthropologists mistakenly believed the skeletons discovered in this valley represented the "missing link" between ape and man. Why? Because of the "primitive" condition in which they were found (i.e., stone tools). Also, the bones seemed to be of a thickness more like apes than humans. **(See fig. #49.)**

Evolutionists have the idea that if a creature lived in a cave, it was subhuman. Yet even today in different parts of the world, many natives live in the most primitive of conditions, but are fully human. They are intelligent, possess the capability of being

Figure #48. MR. NEANDERTHAL

civilized, educated, and speak a highly developed and grammatically complex language.

After the discovery of the first skeleton, several others were also uncovered. From these, evolutionists selected an old, deteriorated skeleton that appeared to be stooped and subhuman. Mr. Neanderthal was reconstructed to appear halfway between ape and man. Hair covered his

Figure #49. HOME SWEET HOME OF THE FIRST MISSING LINK

entire body, his appearance was made to look unkempt, and his head was situated in a thrust forward position making it appear he shuffled along like a baboon. **(See fig. #50.)** Evolutionists felt Neanderthal Man provided evidence that early man didn't walk fully upright, but bent over like an ape. However, the skeleton later was discovered to be that of a diseased elderly person. That is why the bones appeared to be subhuman. The disease caused curvature of the spine; otherwise, it could have been a modern intelligent human. **(See fig. #51.)**

The Rest of the Story.

For decades, evolutionists suggested that this "missing link" lived 80,000 to 1,000,000 years ago (depending upon which book you read). However, recently it has been discovered that Neanderthal was not much different from modern man.

Since the original discoveries of the first Neanderthals in Europe, a large number of skeletal remains have been uncovered in the caves and ancient burial grounds throughout Europe as well as of Asia and Africa. These have been classified, for evolutionary purposes, as ancient men of the Neanderthal race. **(See fig. #52.)**

They have confirmed that these ancient people were not stooped over nor did they have curvature of the spine. In other words, they stood up straight. When the first skeleton was re-examined, it was

Figure #50. MR. COOL DUDE

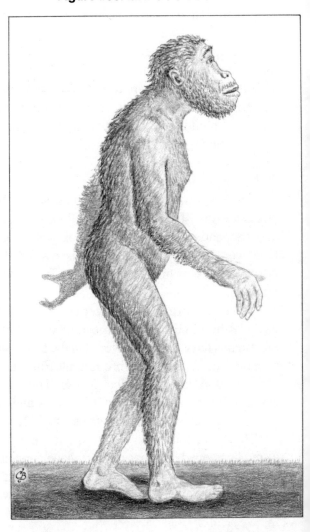

Figure #51. APE-MAN OR AN ELDERLY PERSON?

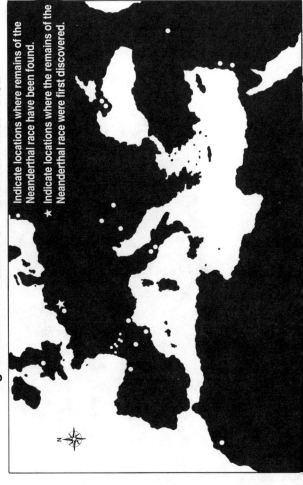

Figure #52. THE HOMES OF NEANDERTHAL RACE

found the spine was curved due to a bad case of arthritis. **(See fig. #53.)** Research has revealed that the somewhat brutish appearance of some of these ancient people was due to bone disease (rickets, arthritis). They contracted these diseases because of a vitamin D deficiency as a result of the cold, damp and poorly sunlit climatic characteristics of their regions at that time.

Present Day "Neanderthals."

Even today some people have a congenital deformity that leaves them with a modified brain capacity. These cases are not seen by the public, as the sufferers are usually confined to medical centers. I have observed some of these sad situations, and I own a medical book which depicts numerous unusual deformities.[14] Some do have ape-like characteristics, but they are not apemen, missing links nor transitional forms. They are simply human beings who unfortunately have a physical deformity. I wonder what claims would be made if the skulls of these people living today were retrieved in the Olduvai Gorge. This gorge in East Africa has become famous because it is where some incredible claims have been made during recent years regarding finds of so-called ape-man-like transitional forms.

Figure #53. SKELETAL DISEASES/RICKETS— NORMAL

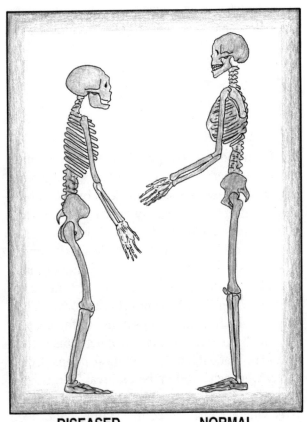

DISEASED **NORMAL**

Chapter Fifteen

The Elephant Man

(See fig. #54.)
A Twenty-First Century Disorder.

John Merrick, born in England in 1862, had an enormous and deformed head. A large, bony mass projected outward from where his eyebrows should have been. His upper lip protruded and turned outward. His right side, arm and leg were unusually thick. This was the result of having a hereditary disease called neurofibromatosis — a thickening of the nerve endings, which causes fibroid tumors. This disorder affects about 50 of every 100,000 people, some more severly than others. If the spine is affected, curvature of the spine results. John Merrick, who became known as the Elephant Man, had a severe case of curvature of the spine.

The First Neanderthals.

The first Neanderthals discovered were from

Figure #54. A CASE OF NEUROFIBROMATOSIS

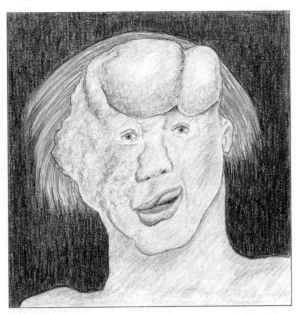

harsh inland environments in Europe. They could have suffered easily like many of our own American Indians from diseases which caused skeletal abnormalities. These diseases resulted from a lack of iodine in the diet and a shortage of sun-induced vitamin D. This is necessary for the absorption of calcium during long winters such as those which would have occurred during the Ice Age after Noah's Flood. There is a physical disorder known as acromegaly, which produces a thickening of the bones and is caused by a pituitary tumor. This enlargement of the skeletal frame can cause one to appear grotesque, even ape-like, but does not affect one's intelligence in the least. People who suffer from neurofibromatosis and other such diseases are certainly not ape-men, and neither were the Neanderthals.

Chapter Sixteen

Neanderthal's Relatives

(See fig. #55.)
Cro-Magnon Man.

Another group of fossils has been found across Europe. These remains have been dubbed the Cro-Magnon ethnic group. They were taller, better built, and had a much larger brain size than modern Europeans. **(See fig. #56.)** Neanderthals averaged about five feet five inches in height, while Cro-Magnons were taller — reaching more than six feet in height.

Despite a Cro-Magnon's greater cranial capacity, he would go virtually unnoticed in a city today. In fact, give Mr. Neanderthal and Mr. Cro-Magnon a shave and they wouldn't appear out of the ordinary on any American street. In fact, the hairstyles of some of today's youth seem to indicate that evolutionism is going in reverse. Even if we left the hair on the faces of these early humans they would still fit into the unkempt

Figure #55. CRO-MAGNON MAN

Figure #56. NEANDERTHAL'S RELATIVES
BRAIN SIZES OF FOSSIL AND MODERN HUMAN BEINGS

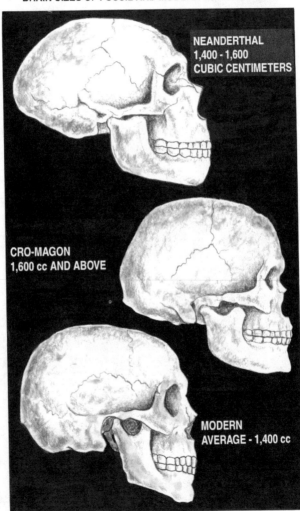

macho styles commonly seen in our large cities.

Besides the larger specimens of Cro-Magnon and Neanderthal, fossils reveal that some ancient people were small in stature, averaging around five feet in height. But that is meaningless since there are people today whose average height is less than that of these ancient peoples. The Negritos of Oceania have an average height of 4'8 feet, and the Pygmies of the highlands of New Guinea stand between 4'9" and 5'1" feet in height. The variation in height and brain sizes observed in fossil humans can be found in today's population. The various types of early men simply show that God created a great variety of types within the human species. An article in the *Smithsonian* magazine was entitled, "Cro-Magnon Hunters Were Really Us Working Out Strategies for Survival." Now if they were us, they could not have evolved into us!

Chapter Seventeen

A Face-Lift for the Neanderthals and a Change of Face for the Evolutionists

(See fig. #57.)
The Evolutionary Community Agrees.

The picture of the dull-witted, shuffling, frowning Neanderthal was popular until recently. Now, as one evolutionist has written,

> Most paleoanthropologists and the artists working under their direction have given the Neanderthals a shower and a shave and straightened up their shoulders. Neanderthal men and women no longer shuffle along on bent legs, staring vacantly. Now they stride erect and with purpose — not exactly like us in the face, but clearly a race of our own kind. (Rensberger, 1981)

A Face-Lift for the Neanderthals and a Change of Face for the Evolutionists

Figure #57. NEANDERTHAL'S FACE-LIFT

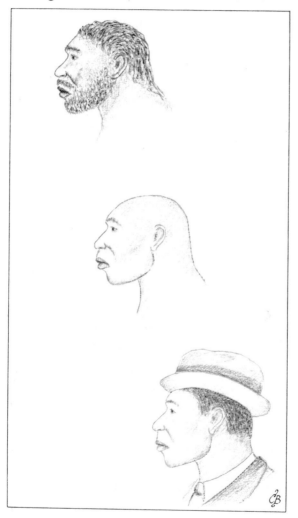

The *Encyclopedia Britannica* (15th edition) states the following in its segment entitled *Neanderthal Man*:

> The popular conception that those people were slouched in posture and walked with a shuffling, bent-kneed gait seems to have been due in large part to faulty reconstruction of the skull base and to misinterpretation of certain features of the limb bones of one of the Neanderthal skeletons discovered early in the 20th century.

Unfortunately, the evolutionary community forgot to mention to the editors of *Time* magazine that they had changed their minds about Neanderthal being the missing link. In the cover story of an issue in 1977, entitled *How Man Became Man* (11/7/77), the writer states that the facts have begun to roll in to support evolutionism. He refers to Neanderthal Man, Java Man and Peking Man. The editors must have been living in some isolated cave in Lower Swabovia (near Upper Swabovia); these three fellows had at the time already been discarded as possible ancestors of man by most in the evolutionary community.

What Changed the Evolutionists' Minds?

Today even evolutionary paleoanthropologists agree that the Neanderthals were human beings who lived in Europe, not the supposed missing link. Why have they come to this conclusion that is so different from what they first believed? Why the face-lift for the Neanderthals and the change of face for the evolutionists? The answer is very simple: The overwhelming evidence demands it.

Interestingly, the evidence regarding Neanderthal Man supports the Bible. For one thing, these men were concerned for life, and even life after death. They buried their dead wearing robes, boots, belts, coats and hats along with flowers and art. In fact, in one grave there were iron arrowheads and a suit of chain mail armor over the skeleton.[15] Their artwork is considered exceptional. Much of it was done in red, black and brown, and because of the almost complete absence of light in the caves where the artwork was found, the colors are as vivid as if they were recently applied. Not many today could duplicate their work **(see fig. #58)**. They also used flint tools, like the American Indian did only a century ago. As one evolutionist, Sir Arthur Keith, stated:

In size of brain, Neanderthal was not a low form. His skill as a flint artisan shows that his abilities were not those of a low order. He had fire at his command. He buried his dead. He had a distinct and highly evolved form of culture. Neanderthal was certainly not a dawn form of humanity.[16]

Figure #58. CAVEMAN ART

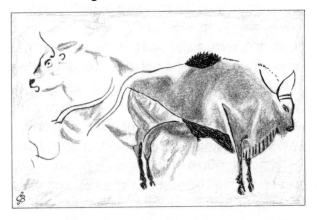

Depending on one's evolutionary bias, the skull cap of Mr. Neanderthal could either resemble an ape-like creature or Marquis de Lafayette — a revolutionary war hero. **(See fig. #59.)**

A Face-Lift for the Neanderthals and a Change of Face for the Evolutionists

Figure #59. MARQUIS DE LAFAYETTE

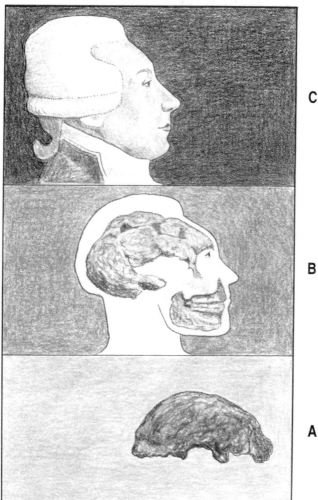

The Lie Lingers On.

Even though the evolutionists have finally admitted that these cavemen are not a "missing link," the public has not been properly informed and still holds to the concept. Museums have removed the old exhibits and replaced them with new exhibits that make the Neanderthal people look very human. The Neanderthal fairy tale has ended up with an unhappy ending for evolutionism. It has turned out to be one more "missing link" that is still missing. However, evolutionists insist that the ABCs of evolutionism must be taught. They are sure that if they search long and hard enough, evidence of the ape-man will be found to support their evolutionary alphabet.

Chapter Eighteen

The Iceman of the Ice Age

(See fig. #60.)
A Recent Discovery.

There is much evidence that humans lived near the edge of an ice sheet in Europe. Creationists believe this sheet of ice originated at the time of Noah's Flood.[17] It was in these higher latitudes that the Neanderthal peoples lived during the Ice Age.

In the summer of 1991 in Western Austria, a mummified body of a man was discovered by hikers on a glacier's edge at about 10,000 feet above sea level. Konrad Spindler of the University of Innsbruck states, "We are absolutely sure this body is 4,000 years old." How can such an exact date be determined? Did they find a driver's license on the man, giving his date of birth? If a note of skepticism is detected, it is because I know the body was only assigned an age of 4,000 years. Otherwise, because they had much more evidence than usual on which to base

Figure #60. THE ICEMAN

This illustration is based upon original design created by artist John Gurche.

their conclusions they would have assigned it as being 10,000, 20,000 or 50,000 old. After all, according to evolutionists, man has been around for at least one or two million years, and the Ice Age extended far beyond 4,000 years ago.

The reason they assigned this man's age at 4,000 years is that the ice had preserved the man, his clothing, and the rest of what he was carrying very well. The implements he was carrying were a bronze axe, a flint knife, a woodframed backpack, a bow, arrows and a quiver. His clothing was made of leather, chamois, fur, and he wore a leather necklace. He had several tattoos, and a close inspection revealed he shaved and cut his fingernails.

Had not Mr. Iceman and his possessions been so well preserved no doubt he would have been assigned an age of 100,000 years or more.

As a result of their findings, investigators studying the Iceman's remains were forced to rethink their standard evolutionary assumptions. Professor Konrad Spindler of the University of Innsbruck had to admit:

> This was no primitive savage. He was very well-nourished, strong and well-dressed. If I passed him on the mountain, I would feel moved to greet him very politely and very respectfully.[18]

Ancient Contemporaries of the Neanderthals.

There is no reason why these isolated cultures like the Neanderthals could not have been contemporary with the advanced civilizations of Egypt, China, Babylonia and others that were developing in the lower latitudes nearer to the equator after Noah's Flood. It is very likely that the Ice Age lasted only a few hundred years, rather than two million years as evolutionists believe. (The biblical perspective of the Ice Age is covered in Volume VI of the Creation Science Series.) The Ice Age occurred at the time of Noah's Flood and lingered on for several centuries afterward.

The Iceman was simply another member of the human race. Like the Neanderthals and the Cro-Magnon ethnic groups, he was one of the descendants of Noah who spread out across the Earth after the dispersion of the races. The division of the people into nations occurred as a result of the rebellion. It happened at the time of the construction of the Tower of Babel (see Gen. 11).

Because of the people's evil purpose to glorify man rather than God, He separated them into races, languages and ethnic groups. He did this to slow down the progress of evil. Today, evil is again spreading very rapidly. It is the result of many of Earth's people speaking a common language, English, and because the use of computers allows us to store and retrieve tremendous amounts of knowledge. The time is drawing near when God will once again separate the peoples of the world. Some are attempting to unify all peoples with another "Tower of Babel" — the United Nations. This time God will divide mankind into two groups: the godly and the ungodly. He will judge the wicked and reward those who have made Him Lord.

> All the nations will be gathered before him, and he will separate the people one from another as a shepherd separates the sheep from the goats (Matt. 25:32).

Chapter Nineteen

Variety Within the Human Species

Variety is Indicative of God's Creation.

In the book *Early Man*,[19] the last four drawings in the ape-man chart are considered fully human by the evolutionary community, though they see each type as slowly evolving. **(See fig. #61.)**

However, from a creation point of view, these creatures are simply varieties of the human species. God created man with the potential to develop a host of different physical characteristics — earlobes, skin color, hair texture, and many more.

In modern times we see amazing variety in humans and all other creatures. But according to Scripture, what we see today is nothing compared to the diversity that was present when man and all the other creatures were created. Since

Variety Within the Human Species

Figure #61. HOMO SAPIENS NOT HOMO SIMIANS

RHODESIAN MAN

NEANDERTHAL MAN

CRO-MAGNON MAN

MODERN MAN

the curse took effect, there has been a slow but steady extinction of all creatures.

Figure #62A. YOUR ORDER PLEASE: SAPIEN OR SIMIAN

A

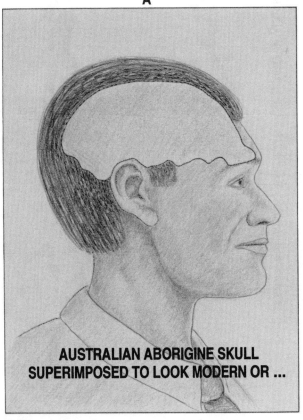

AUSTRALIAN ABORIGINE SKULL SUPERIMPOSED TO LOOK MODERN OR ...

Variety Within the Human Species

Jim Thorpe, a famous athlete, possessed physical features almost identical to those of Mr. Neanderthal. There are many races of men on **Figure #62B.**

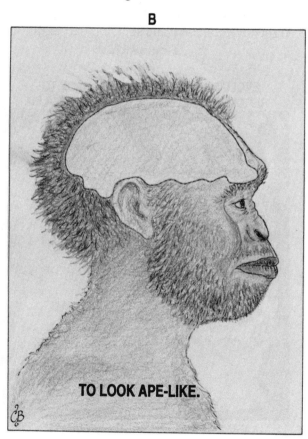

TO LOOK APE-LIKE.

Earth even today who possess the same sloping forehead as Rhodesia Man — another early man that apparently was a part of an ethnic group which has become extinct. Variation is normal and changes can occur rather quickly, given the right environmental and sociological conditions.

Figure #62C.

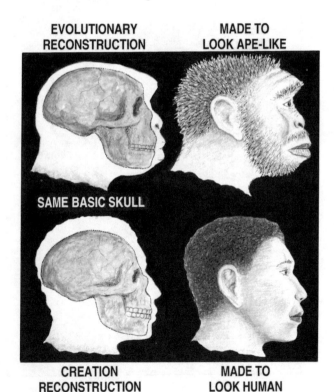

Changes Today.

For example, the average size of a male Japanese skull prior to World War II was just over 900 cubic centimeters. Today it is 1400 cc — a result of improved heath care, nourishment and exercise.[20] Rapid change within a culture is common. The average height of the American male has jumped several inches since World War II. This is obvious in the sport of basketball. In the 60s, a seven-foot player was a spectacle. Today it is quite common to see a seven-foot player, and most professional NBA teams have two or more.

As it can be seen, because of the guesswork involved in the reconstruction of a skull, it can end up looking ape-like or human. All the artist has to do is change the flesh parts of the face to fashion whatever the look he desires. **(See figs. #62A,B,C.)** Thus the idea that unusual skeletal forms are evidence of the evolutionary process of man is simply a tale even a fairy wouldn't tell! In spite of evidence that continues to reveal the truth that the ABCs of evolutionism are nothing more than an adult fantasy, the search goes on. Skull 1470, Lucy and the australopithecines are up next. They represent the best that evolutionism has to offer. Their stories are as incredulous as those previously covered.

PART IV
OLDEST MAN OR FOSSIL APE (HOMOHABULUS)?

Chapter 20: Skull 1470

Chapter 21: Dating the World's Oldest Man

Chapter 22: How Apes Become Human

Chapter Twenty

Skull 1470

(See fig. #63)
1470 and 1968.

The name of Richard Leakey, the prominent anthropologist, has been mentioned several times in the preceding chapters. Now we shall take an in-depth look into his rise to stardom. It centers around the discovery of a skull that has become known as Skull 1470, and it all began in 1968.

"Don't Call Us; We'll Call You."

Before Dr. Richard Leakey went to Africa in 1968, he met with the research committee of the National Geographic Society, and asked for money to finance his search for ape-men. The research committee agreed to give him the money but stipulated: "If you find nothing, you are never to come begging at our door again."[21] In other words, "Put up or shut up."

Figure #63. SKULL 1470

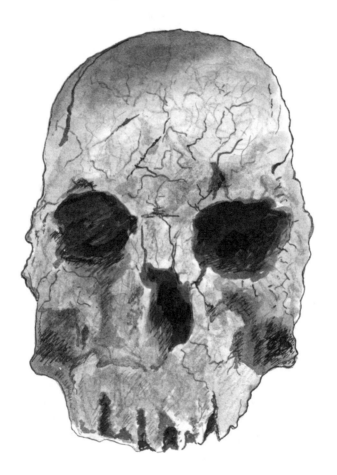

The Emergence of Homohabulus.[22]

With such encouraging words, it was evident that "lady luck" would bless Leakey. It was not long before he had found enough bones to gain him popularity. His native helpers discovered some additional bone fragments that had been washed down the side of a gully. Leakey collected a bag full of these pieces, and the reconstruction began. Within six weeks, one of Leakey's skulls became world news. Homohabulus (meaning *the first handyman*) put Richard Leakey in the big leagues. His discovery became known as Skull 1470 (the assigned registration number which identifies it at the Kenya National Museum in East Rudolph).

Skull 1470 was popularly portrayed by the media as the "oldest man," dated at 2.6 million years. *National Geographic* (6/73) covered the story of its emergence in detail.

What was So Unusual About Skull 1470?

How was Skull 1470 any different from the other skulls? The primary reason Homohabulus was placed into the lineage of man was because its skull was *exactly* like that of modern man except much smaller. The brain capacity of Leakey's reconstruction Skull 1470 was 800 cc — much larger than that of skulls previously discovered in Africa, but considerably smaller than skulls of modern adults, which are 1200 to 1500 cc.

However, it is not known whether the skull was that of a child or an adult, a male or female. And today there are aboriginal skulls the size of Skull 1470.

Furthermore, John Harris, who has been associated with the National Museum of Kenya, found human bones nearby in the same layer of strata that Skull 1470 was found, and the bones are similar to human bones today. This immediately raises the question as to why Skull 1470 was considered a transitional link rather than human since it has all the characteristics of being fully human. Depending on the artist, Skull 1470 can be made to look like an ape or human or anything in between. It all depends on how one fills in the skull with muscle, skin and tissue. **(See fig. #64.)**

Skull 1470 was thought by evolutionists to be a transitional link because they believe that 2.6 million years ago only ape-men existed. Supposedly, man was just becoming man at that time. That only makes sense if one is an evolutionist. How do we know that Skull 1470 is 2.6 million years old? Answer: Evolutionism. How does evolutionism know that Skull 1470 is 2.6

Figure #64. BEAUTY OR BEAST DEPENDS ON THE ARTIST

SKULL 1470

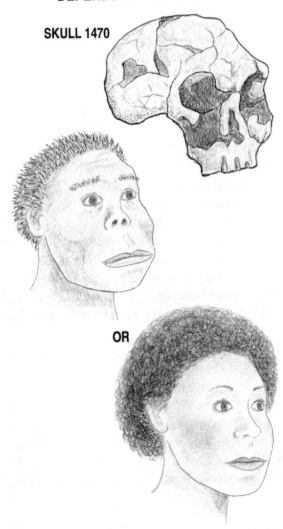

OR

Skull 1470

million years old? Answer: The volcanic rock around where the skull was found was dated to be 2.6 million years old by the dating process known as Radio Active Potassium Argon (K-AR). Sounds like reasonable proof, doesn't it? Let's take a closer look at the wrinkles surrounding Skull 1470 and see if he is as old as evolutionists say he is. There are wrinkles, but not on Mr. 1470's face. The wrinkles are in the manner by which he was dated.

Chapter Twenty-One

Dating the World's Oldest Man

How Old is Mr. 1470?

Many think radioactive dating is a foolproof method of determining a rock's age. Richard Leakey's experience with Skull 1470 shows otherwise. When Leakey made his find, he believed the skull was about 2.6 million years old. He arrived at this date based on the type of rock in which Skull 1470 was found. The type of rock and the layer in which it was discovered was then compared to the evolutionary timetable.

Leakey sent samples of volcanic ash which had surrounded Skull 1470 to London for dating. Using the potassium-argon method of dating, the samples didn't give the estimated 2.6 million years but rather an incredible date of 220 million years — an impossibly high figure for the emergence of man's ancestors according to the evolutionary time chart.

More samples were sent, and more unacceptable dates were given. They ranged from 290,000 to 19 million years. Can you guess the date that was finally picked to be the "right" one? You guessed it — 2.6 million years, and this is the date now used for Mr. 1470. How do you suppose Dr. Leakey guessed so accurately? Evolutionists kept trying until they arrived at a date which matched the evolutionary time chart. Any date to the contrary was considered contaminated and thus of no value.

How Reliable Is K-AR?

In 1973, tree roots were fossilized within moments when a high voltage line fell near Grand Prairie, Alberta, Canada. Scientists at the University of Regina, Saskatchewan, were asked what the results would be if these root specimens were dated by K-AR. They stated that the test "would be meaningless."

Why would it be meaningless? Because it would indicate an age of millions of years as a result of heat being involved in the petrification process. Did you grasp that? When heat is involved in the radiometric dating process, it becomes meaningless. Normally, evolutionism believes that fossilization takes place under a slow and gradual process of being covered by dirt, where no extreme heat is involved. Similarly, one cannot discover a room's true temperature if the thermometer is located just above the radiator. The same is true when dating rocks which have been affected by heat; so what about all the volcanic ash found around fossils?

Famous "Ape-Men."

In light of the discrepancies in the rocks' ages, due to the untrustworthy methods used, it might be noted that the following famous evolutionary discoveries were all "dated" by the radiometric test with volcanic (ash) material overlying the actual artifacts.

1. "Lucy" dated at three million years old (*Nationall Geographic. 12/76*)
2. Footprints of Lucy's relatives dated at 3.6 million years old (*Nationall Geographic. 4/79*)
3. Australopithecus-Ethiopia was publicized as being 1- to 2- million years old by K-AR dating for the overlying rocks. However, mammal bones in the same deposit produced a C-14 date of 15,000 years old.
4. Zinjanthropus was dated by potassium-argon at 1.75 million years. Someone else dated the mammal bones from the same bed which Zinjanthropus was discovered

using C-14 and the bones gave a date of only 10,000 years.

The question is, "Which method was right or were they both wrong?"[23]

The Great Temptation.

The public has a great appetite for the sensational. That is one reason scientists face a great temptation to use a unique process (such as radiometric dating) in order to ascertain a date that takes their work from interesting to sensational. There is an even greater temptation for a scientist to selectively choose a date when he thinks his professional reputation and the influence and affluence that come with it are at stake. Remember how the National Geographic Society instructed Dr. Leakey before they funded his expedition to Africa? "Put up or shut up."

It is not hard, to understand how easy it is to give in to the temptation to "manufacture" a sensational story, especially when it will mean remaining in good standing with a prestigious organization such as the National Geographic Society, which has been providing the funds for one's research.

Chapter Twenty-Two

How Apes Become Human

Additional Insight on the Emergence of Homo habulus.

Author John Reader has provided insight into how an ape fossil can acquire its "humanness."[24] In September 1973, Richard Leakey announced a meeting with the scientific community to discuss his conclusions about Skull 1470. Attending the meeting were anthropologists Bernard Wood, Dr. Alan Walker of the Johns Hopkins School of Medicine and Michael Day. According to Mr. Reader, the meeting didn't run smoothly.

Leakey and Wood stated that Skull 1470 seemed to have a "large brain" for the overall size of the skull and therefore must be "Homo" (fully man), an ancestor of man. However, Dr. Alan Walker, who was the scientist mostly involved with the reconstruction of Skull 1470's fossil fragments, argued that the skull had similarities to the australopithecine (southern apes) and that brain size had nothing to do with the reasoning.

The debate heated up, and there was no compromise from either side. Finally, Dr. Walker stated that if a published description of Skull 1470 was to include any reference of being man, his name must be removed from the paper. He was concerned for his academic standing and the status of his contributions to the field of anthropology.

The squabble continued and a statement was made that Dr. Walker's withdrawal might be welcomed. At this point Dr. Walker left the room. Although the paper was finally published with both names endorsing the contents of the article, the two have never fully come to an agreement regarding the intelligence of Skull 1470. Was he or wasn't he human? Apparently, only his Creator knows.

Nevertheless, Leakey called it homo habilis, even though Dr. Walker classified the skull as simply another australopithecine, or ape. The skull has for all intents and purposes simply dropped out of public sight. Why? Probably for one of two reasons: If it was as close to being human as some claimed, it was of little use to the evolutionist as a "missing link." Another ape skull was no help either in the search for the "missing link."

Richard's Roots.

Richard Leakey and his father, Louis, came from a family with a very rich Christian heritage. Richard's grandparents were Anglican missionaries to Kenya.

Richard related that he decided against Christianity when he was punished for arriving late at a Christian school, though his tardiness was the result of a bicycle accident. Such an excuse reveals the heart of the matter. The problem isn't with Christianity; it is with Richard who wants to be king.

It is sad to see a man of science, or anyone for that matter, reject his Creator and labor so diligently to prove He does not exist. And all for what? To proclaim that man is the result of an accident. Why would a person wish to spend his entire life trying to prove that? If there is no purpose for our being here, what purpose is there in the future? Evolutionists try to convince us that life came into existence totally by accident; there was no thought behind it; it just happened. If it were to happen again, man might not "evolve." They make up the story as they go along, with no rhyme nor reason on which to base it. Now that we humans are here, we really have no future. What a waste! It's difficult to understand how an intelligent person could believe this pagan fairy tale, but it is impossible to comprehend why a person would spend all of his life's energy looking for evidence to prove such absurdity. God's Word tells us that the fool says in his heart, "There is no God" (Psa. 14:1).

PART V
EVOLUTIONISM'S MOST PRESTIGIOUS APE-MEN AND APE-WOMEN

Chapter 23: Australopithecines (1924)

Chapter 24: Zinjanthropus (Mr. Z) (1959)

Chapter 25: An Ape Named Lucy — Ape-Woman of the Year (1975)

Chapter 26: Lucy's Ludicrous Legacy Lingers On

Chapter 27: I Love Lucy: The Ludicrous Lucy Legacy Lives On

Chapter 28: Fossil Footprints: A Final Footnote

Chapter 29: Evolutionism's Pagan Religion

Chapter Twenty-Three

Australopithecines (1924)

(See fig. #65.)
Apes from the South

Australopithecus is a 24-carat label given to an assortment of bone fragments claimed to be another link in the long line of missing links that make up the missing chain. The name means "southern ape," and no doubt that is all that it is — an ape from the south (Australo = southern, pithicus = ape). It is pronounced *aw-stra-lo-pi-the-kuss*. "An awful and pitiful cuss" might be a better name for this "missing link." This creature became number one on the evolutionary "missing link" chart, and in 1975 was crowned ape-woman of the year.

The first australopithecine was the result of a skull discovered by Dr. Raymond Dart in 1924 in South Africa. Dr. Dart believed that although the skull he uncovered was ape-like, the teeth he found were more human-like than those found in modern apes.

Figure #65. AUSTRALOPITHECUS

Microtechnology.

A pebble was found near the skull, and evolutionists claimed it was a tool — the final confirmation they needed for australopithecus' credentials as a creature on its way to becoming man. This southern ape was not only advancing in technology, but apparently he was into micro-technology because the size of the so-called tool is about the size of a jelly bean! One of the best ways to tell it is a tool is the museum number stamped on it. So Dr. Dart announced to the world that this creature was on its way to becoming human. However, many of his evolutionary colleagues disagreed with him, claiming that this "southern ape" was nothing more than an ape from the south. This of course didn't persuade him.

Dart's Fan Club Grows.

In time, Dr. Dart's fan club grew as more and more evolutionists were attracted to the fantasy. Another australopithecine (set of similar bones) was found and named "Robustus," meaning a strong and hardy ape from the south. It was reconstructed from head-to-toe from several craniums, more than a dozen jaws and hundreds of teeth found in *two* South African caves. It is my guess that in order to do this incredibly tricky reconstruction, the men would have needed the medical and dental records of one of these creatures in order to prevent incorrect pieces from being attached to Mr. Australopithecus.

In 1959, famous anthropologist Dr. Louis Leakey and his wife, Mary, discovered a cousin of australopithecus in Tanzania. He was dubbed East Africa Man or Mr. Zinjanthropus, and overnight Dr. Leakey became famous for his discovery.

Before we take a closer look at Mr. Z in the next chapter, it should be noted that Richard, the son of Dr. and Mrs. Leakey, was a prominent anthropologist in the evolutionary community. In his book, *Human Origins*, he removed australopithecus from the ape-man chart and time line in *Time* (8/7/77), and put him in a line all of his own. Richard doesn't believe australopithecus is one of man's ancestors.

He believes the australopithecus came from the remains of an extinct ape that lived in South Africa. In chapter one we recounted the record of the battle between Dr. Richard Leakey and his Skull 1470 and Dr. Johanson and his australopithecine, Lucy. In this chapter we see that Louis Leakey and his son, Richard, were at odds over australopithecus. The battle over "missing links" still rages — even among the evolutionists themselves.

Chapter Twenty-Four

Zinjanthropus (Mr. Z) (1959)

(See fig. #66.)
400-Piece Perplexing Paleontologist Puzzle.

In 1959, *National Geographic* captured the public's attention with the ape-man Zinjanthropus (Zinj = East Africa, and anthropus = man). This 400-piece puzzle was assembled from skull fragments. Since the pieces didn't fit very well, a lot of guesswork went into it. As a result, the assembled Mr. Zinjanthropus looked as though a 3-year-old child had glued together the pieces.

Will the Real Mr. Z Please Stand Up?

The evidence was so scanty that various artistic impressions of Mr. Z were created to cover all possibilities as to how he might have looked. **(See fig. #67.)**

Four different artists' renditions of Mr. Australopithecus Boisei[25] reveal the vague and

Figure #66. 400-PIECE PUZZLE: A CRANIUM CRACK-UP

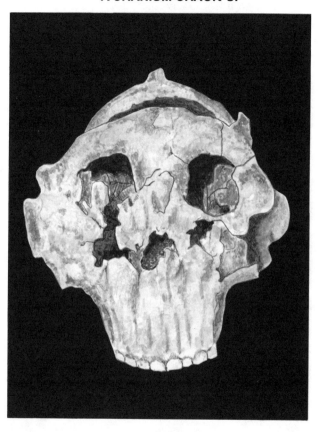

speculative nature of evolutionary imaginations. The truth is, a person often "sees" evidence that supports his belief, even though the evidence

Figure #67. WILL THE REAL MR. Z PLEASE STAND UP?

doesn't really exist. He also fails to see or pays little attention to anything that contradicts what he believes.

One additional bit of interesting information is concerning the bones found *below* the resting place of Mr. Zinjanthropus. Supposedly, a more modern man was found. Does this mean that modern man sired an ape-man? Evolutionists always have explanations for such discrepancies. Nevertheless, Mr. Zinjanthropus is a pretty weak link in evolutionism's missing chain. In fact, today he has been demoted to an ape because of the grossly ape-like characteristics. Mr. Z isn't considered to be related to man at all. But the kangaroo court convenes from time to time in an attempt to discover who his real relatives are. It appears Mr. Z does have one relative; her name is Lucy. She received her name when she was discovered by anthropologist, Donald Carl Johanson and his party while listening to the Beatles' hit tune of the 1960s, "Lucy in the Sky with Diamonds." The fantasy continues as evolutionists attempt to link Lucy to Adam (the original man) by "lady luck."

Chapter Twenty-Five

An Ape Named Lucy — Ape-Woman of the Year (1975)

(See fig. #68.)
Lucy's Ludicrous Legacy: Once Upon a Time, Long Long Ago... .

Wait until you hear this wild story! Lucy is a three-and-a-half foot adult skeleton dated at 3.2 million years old. She looks just like the skeleton of a modern chimpanzee, and she weighed only 50 pounds. Lucy comes from the family of australopithecines. The famous American anthropologist, Donald Carl Johanson found some bone fragments (40% of the complete skeleton) in the Afar area of Ethiopia in 1975 and named them Australopithecus Afarensis. **(See fig. #69.)** Johanson declared the bone fragments "Homo," the scientific name for man. Four years later he announced to the world that Lucy's bones were actually those of the most primitive species

Figure #68. APE-WOMAN OF THE YEAR

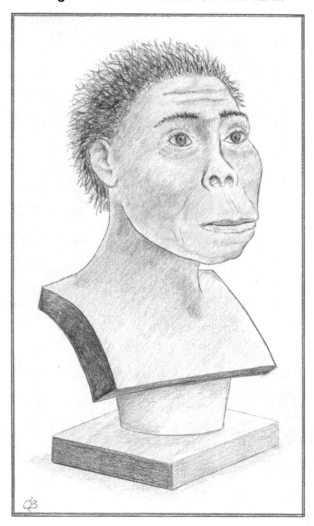

Figure #69. LUCY'S REMAINS

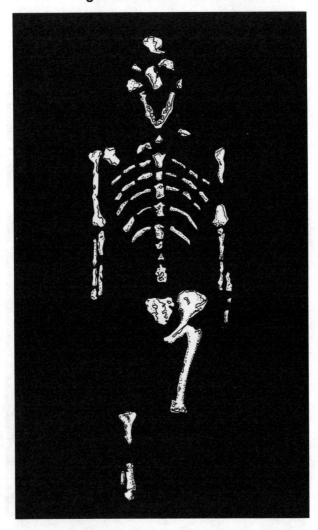

related to man. The story of Johanson's "new discovery" hit the news, and *Time* magazine (1/29/79) provided its usual biased report.

The reason for all the attention was Johanson's statement that 3.2 million years ago, Lucy walked upright like man. Suddenly, there was a new definition of man: any creature who walks upright. Although Johanson admitted that from the neck up, Lucy was ape (she had the jaws, teeth, face and brain of an ape), he still maintained that Lucy walked upright just like a human, and therefore she was on her way to becoming man — or should we say a woman. Did he forget that today the pygmy chimpanzee wanders around in the rain forest walking upright almost all the time? **(See fig. #70.)** The fact that a creature walks upright doesn't prove anything. Is the pygmy chimp on its way to becoming man? Or maybe Lucy is just the ancestor of the pygmy chimpanzee since all the other features of Lucy are ape-like. Chickens walk upright, but they don't produce humans. If you detect a bit of sarcasm, read on and you shall see sarcasm turns into outright ridicule.

Three Bones of Contention.

Everyone agrees that from the neck up Lucy was gorilla-like. The only three bones associated

Figure #70. PYGMY CHIMPANZEE

with Lucy which supposedly show any distinctly human features are:
1. The arm and leg bone ratio (the arm length to the leg length)
2. Left pelvic bone and
3. A knee joint

Arm-Leg Ratio.

In an ape the arm is about as long as

the leg. In a human, the arm is about three-fourths as long the leg. Lucy's arm is listed as precisely 83.9% as long as her leg, placing her somewhere between ape and man. **(See fig. #71.)**

But in making this measurement, Johanson's evolutionary bias was introduced. The leg bone had been broken in two places and one end had been partially crushed. Johanson, by his own admission, *estimated* the leg length. This estimation makes Johnson's "precise" measurement a useless proof.

Lucy's Pelvis.

Lucy's left pelvic bone is complete, but according to Johanson it is distorted. Since Lucy is the only "missing link" of her kind in existence, it is puzzling that the experts claim to know it is distorted — unless, of course, they wish to reshape it until it appears that Lucy walked upright. Other evolutionary scientists, such as Lord Zuckerman and Charles Oxnard, do not believe that Lucy walked upright. Dr. Oxnard, Professor of Anatomy and Director of Graduate Studies at the University of Southern California used a sophisticated computer to analyze Lucy's pelvic bone and concluded Johanson's claims unfounded.[26]

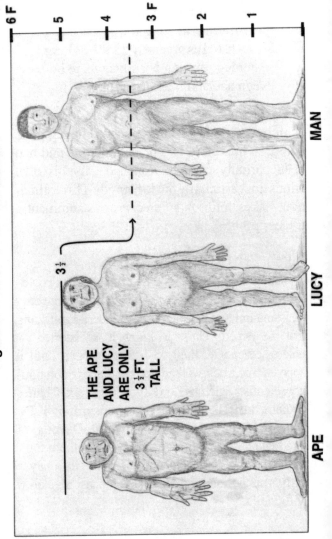

Figure #71. LUCY'S MEASUREMENTS

The Knee Joint.

Actually, the only features of Lucy which even hint that she walked with an erect posture are her knee joints. Humans' knee joints are distinctly different from apes', so these joints indicate how the creature to which they belonged walked. Unfortunately, when presented with the Lucy fantasy, most university students never hear that when Dr. Johanson required a knee joint to prove that Lucy walked upright, he used one found nearly two miles down the road, buried 200 feet deeper than the other bones. Did you comprehend that? Lucy's knee joint had walked away from the rest of her bone fragments. How many evolutionary books do you suppose contain this bit of devastating information? If there is one, it most likely will be written by an evolutionist who wishes to discredit Johanson in order to make a name for himself. When questioned about the distance between Lucy's knee joint and the rest of her bone fragments and how he was so sure the knee joint was Lucy's, Johanson replied, "anatomical similarity," meaning it seemed to fit and looked like it was a part.

How is that for convincing evidence that Lucy walked upright and was on her way to womanhood? If this is science, then we are still living in the Dark Ages. This isn't comical; it's absurd. What is laughable is that evolutionists claim that creation science isn't scientific. Clearly, the knee is not Lucy's, but even if it were, it has not been proven diagnostically to belong to a creature who walked upright. In fact, it more likely belongs to a tree-climbing creature, according to Dr. Oxnard and other authorities.

Another Look.
A. The ratio of the arm length to the leg length
   1. Ape: equal length
   2. Man: arm 3/4 as long as leg length
   3. Lucy: 83.9% as long as leg length (not: 80, 85, or 84 but 83.9%)
B. Left pelvic bone
   1. Distorted
   2. Rejected by other evolutionists
C. A knee joint found
   1. 200 ft. below
   2. Two miles away

Johanson misrepresented the evidence. And most likely he did so for fame and fortune. If a businessman made claims like this to sell his products, he would be charged with fraud rather than be paid an honorarium when invited to share such an unfounded assumption. As an anthropologist, Johanson is fully aware that a large hip joint does not prove upright posture, neither does it prove higher intelligence nor the ability to beget a human. Here we have another case of a proud father who will not confront the facts about his "child." The result is belief in science fiction or monkey mythology. Lucy has a long way to go before "lady luck" can link her with Adam and Eve.

Chapter Twenty-Six

Lucy's Ludicrous Legacy Lingers On

The Authorities Speak.

There is much debate regarding whether or not Lucy did in fact walk upright. Dr. Zuckerman, a famous British anatomist, and previously the head of the Department of Anatomy at the University of Birmingham in England, led a team of scientists who studied the skeletal bones of various Australopithecines over a period of 15 years. They used the most sophisticated methods of research. Can you guess what they concluded? Australopithecines did *not* walk upright. Furthermore, they concluded that these fellows were *not* the "missing link" between ape and man, but apes. Dr. Zuckerman even made a startling admission in his book *Beyond the Ivory Tower* that there is no evidence in the fossil record for man evolving from an ape-like creature.[27]

Dr. Charles Oxnard wrote an article in *American Biology Teacher* (5/79) which states that although,

> ... this is the view that is presented in almost all textbooks ... and it is widely broadcast in publications such as the *Time-Life Series* and the beautiful TV story of *The Ascent of Man*; however, anatomical features in some of the these fossils provide a warning against a too-ready acceptance of this story ...

As part of his warning, Dr. Oxnard reminds readers of the blunders once made in such cases as Mr. Piltdown and Mr. Nebraska. In his 1987 book, *Fossils, Teeth and Sex,* Oxnard provides an excellent summary of these various studies. Although Dr. Oxnard is not a creationist, he has declared that these chaps did not walk upright like humans; they were not transitional forms between apes and man, and were not the ancestors of man. He makes a real switch: He suggests that Lucy may have arrived on the scene from modern humans. Upon looking at the behavior and jargon of some children today, it seems he may have a viable and convincing argument.

More from Richard Leakey.

The famous anthropologist, Richard Leakey, admitted that evolutionists do not know whether or not australopithecus walked upright because so far no one has discovered a complete skeleton with an australopithecus skull. It is necessary to know exactly how the spine is attached at the base of the skull in order to be able to accurately interpret the upright condition.[28] Richard Leakey also stated that Lucy's skull was so incomplete that most of it was "imagination, made of plaster of Paris." Richard and others are now claiming that in all likelihood, Lucy is really a mosaic of two or more species. Yet she is still touted as one of the best "evidences" for human evolution.

Remember, this creature was three feet six inches tall, weighed 50 pounds, had long arms, short legs and is believed by many paleontologists to have been a "knuckle-walker." Its skeletal features are virtually indistinguishable from a chimpanzee! What is still a mystery to evolutionists is why in the world did the chimpanzee continue as a chimpanzee and our supposed ape ancestor become man?

More Monkey Mythology.

For the answer as to why the chimp began to walk upright in the first place, we find another amusing tale in the evolutionary book of myths.

> As the earth continued to warm, there was a slow disappearance of the forests. The chimps had fewer and fewer trees to swing; therefore, they had to begin shuffling along on the hot ground. Since the air nearer the ground is warmer than a foot or two above, the apes concluded they should begin standing and walking upright. They also realized the sun doesn't penetrate as much of their bodies when they are standing.[29]

There we have it folks: another lesson straight from the annals of evolutionism, or should we say fantasyland.

The diversionary games to which evolutionists resort to keep God out of the picture are amazing. Put God in His rightful position, and such puzzling issues evaporate instantly.

Chapter Twenty-Seven

I Love Lucy: The Ludicrous Lucy Legacy Lives On

Johanson: A Proud Father.

Although men like Oxnard are evolutionists, they provide objective evidence — unlike the men who actually find the fossil remains of creatures. Just as the "I Love Lucy" TV show will no doubt live on for decades to come because of people who are forever bonded to it, Johanson's claims for his Lucy appear to belong in the same category. He loves his Lucy like a proud father loves his child.

Just as a father never sees his children in quite the same light as others do, scientists are sometimes neither completely objective about their "children."

The evolutionist does what every child does with dolls or action figures — he seeks to humanize his fantasy. The evolutionist attempts to humanize his pet theory — attributing to them emotions and reason — just as pet lovers do with their dogs, cats and other pets. For the evolutionist, the purpose of humanizing ape-man is to overthrow the Bible, to remove its Author, and to try to show He is not needed.

Lucy — What Art Thou?

What is Lucy? There is no evidence she is an ancestor of man. She is probably a relative of today's pygmy chimp. When not swinging in the trees, the pygmy chimp frequently walks upright and has striking similarities to Lucy's structure. It is also possible that australopithecines like Lucy are a unique kind of ape-like creature, genetically unrelated to either the present day apes or man, some of which are now extinct.

It is most likely that the australopithecines are no doubt simply an extinct species of apes that are different from modern apes. Their surviving descendants can be found among modern apes.

Holding Up the Branches of the Evolutionary Family Tree.

Lucy and her relatives are part of one of the most important branches in the imaginary, evolutionary family tree of man. The branch is weighed down with so much evidence against it that long since it would have broken off were it not for a host of diehard evolutionists who continue to support it. They keep it propped up, hoping someone will discover a new brace.

The Lucy fantasy is a clear example that evolutionism has nothing whatsoever to do with science. Belief in evolutionism has to do with a humanistic religious viewpoint.

Chapter Twenty-Eight

Fossil Footprints: A Final Footnote

Another Trail of Ape-Man Prints?

In 1979 *National Geographic* reported the discovery by the famous anthropologist, Mary Leakey of a trail of 77 man-like prints in East Africa. In 1980, *Science News* also covered the story.[30] Mary Leakey illustrates how she believes the prints were formed and preserved; then she speculates on the kind of foot that made them. If you examine the article, you will see that the prints look similar to that of modern man. Of course, the creatures making the tracks look like ape-men. **(See fig. #72.)**

Mary Leakey claims that the prints were made by an australopithecine, the supposedly remote ancestor of man who walked upright with a fully human stride 3.6 million years ago. What is interesting is that all reports say "the footprints

Figure #72. FOSSIL FOOTPRINTS

are as human as they can be, as though made by a child today." However, because of the evolutionary bias of the media, a "missing link" always emerges no matter what the discovery. One article reads:

> If you saw a band of australopithecines from a distance, you would see what appears to be a group of humans walking upright. It's only when they got closer that you'd see the ape faces.[31]

The Same Old Story.

In the center of the *National Geographic* article there is a two-page foldout. An artist has recreated an African landscape using a discovery of animal and human tracks. One sees ostriches, rabbits, elephants, giraffes, guinea hens, and acacia trees — and a set of human tracks. The human prints look exactly like those that a person today would make in soft mud. The scene looks like one that would be seen today in certain parts of Africa after a heavy rain shower. All the animals are depicted exactly like those living today. However, to depict the human, the artist put an ape-like looking person. Only the feet look human. The head looks like a loony tunes character from the comic section of the newspaper. How did the artist know what the creature that made the human tracks looked like? Simple! The evolutionists told him what it looked like. How did the evolutionists know what the creature looked like? Very simply, the evolutionists assumed the strata to be 3.5 million years old, and that 3.5 million years ago creatures must have looked like ape-men. That only makes good scientific sense if one believes in the myth of evolutionism. There has never been any creature that has a footprint that comes close to the human footprint. The reason the tracks look human is that they were made by human beings (3.5 million years ago). If you don't believe the evolutionary fairy tale, you won't even have a problem with human tracks being found side by side with dinosaur footprints![32] **(See figs. #73A and B.)** These human-looking footprints are far more indicative of man than the fossil fragments that have been provided by the evolutionary community. If the footprints above were made by humans, evolutionists would have to admit that man existed before his supposed ancestors (missing links).

From the creationist viewpoint, the "humanlike" footprints found along with the dinosaurs' reveal that man was created along with all the other creatures by Creator God. (Human-like

Fossil Footprints: A Final Footnote

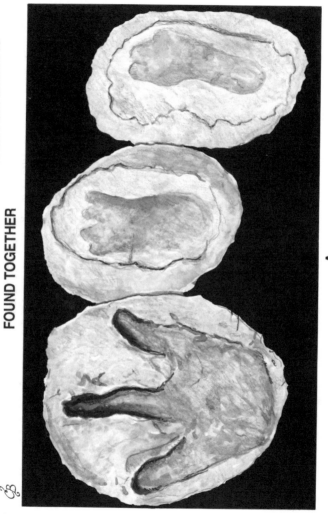

Figure #73A. NEXT DOOR NEIGHBORS: DINOSAURS AND HUMANS FOUND TOGETHER

A

Figure 73B.

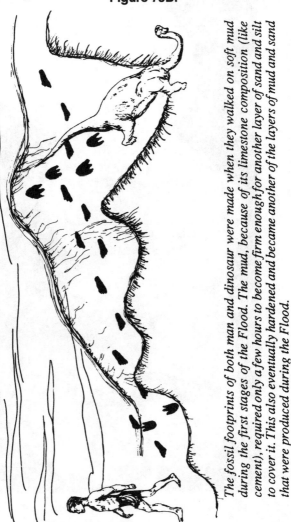

The fossil footprints of both man and dinosaur were made when they walked on soft mud during the first stages of the Flood. The mud, because of its limestone composition (like cement), required only a few hours to become firm enough for another layer of sand and silt to cover it. This also eventually hardened and became another of the layers of mud and sand that were produced during the Flood.

and dinosaur footprints together can be seen in the Paluxy River near Glen Rose, Texas or in casts at ICR's Museum of Creation and Earth History in San Diego, California.

Chapter Twenty-Nine

Evolutionism's Pagan Religion

(See fig. #74.)
The Humanistic Altar Call.

Johanson's conclusions regarding Lucy led him to give a humanistic altar call:

> There is a common ancestor for man and apes, and a common destiny. ... We can now control the destiny not only of ourselves, but of our planet. Join us scientists in controlling our destiny and in bringing about world peace.

Johanson vividly illustrates that evolutionism is simply a widely accepted pagan religion. It is a religion because it requires faith that the gods of time, chance and the environment worked the miracles necessary to build the universe, to create living things, and to help chimpanzees beget humans.

Evolutionism's Pagan Religion

Figure #74. ANCESTRAL WORSHIP

"ALTHOUGH THEY CLAIMED TO BE WISE THEY BECAME FOOLS." (ROM. 1:22)

A Look at Humanism at Its Worst.

The idea that man can control his own destiny is so ludicrous, it hardly necessitates a response. In the last 80 years, communist leaders of the former Soviet Union killed some ten million of their own countrymen. Hitler's Nazis murdered six million Jews and blacks, the Chinese communists — 20 million, the Cambodian communists — three million. And the Americans? Twenty million children have been killed in abortion clinics across the United States. In regard to controlling our own destiny, we have shortened our life expectancy from 900+ years to about 70 years. Our new morality has brought about such amazing life changing treasures as AIDS, herpes, industrial wastes, dioxin and other poisons — all of which should help man to shorten his life span even further. By choice, man is not evolving but *devolving* from a perfect beginning. Evolutionism is more accurately pronounced devolution, or better yet, *evil*ution. Evolutionism is not a science; it is a religion begun by Satan to make fools of men.

> For although they knew God, they neither glorified him as God nor gave thanks to him, but their thinking became futile and their foolish hearts

were darkened. Although they claimed to be wise, they became fools (Rom. 1:21,22).

PART VI
SUCCULENT SWINDLES AND DELECTABLE DECEPTIONS

Chapter 30: National Geographic Society and the Stone Age Swindle

Chapter 31: A Medley of Evolutionary Deceptions

Chapter 32: Escape from Reason

Chapter Thirty

National Geographic Society and the Stone Age Swindle

Evolutionists Taken for a Ride.

There is no letup of the relentless pursuit of evolutionism to find the "missing link." No matter how many setbacks they encounter, they continue to search at any cost. One of the latest evolutionary hoaxes was exposed by the European press. It involved an incredible swindle, and the victims were NBC-TV and the National Geographic Society. It all began in 1971 in Southeast Asia. A hunter named Dafal reported he had discovered a Stone Age tribe of men, women and children living in the thick rain forest of Mindanao, a Philippine island. It wasn't long before the National Geographic Society in Washington was contacted. After NBC became involved, $50,000 was paid in order to have exclusive rights to the story. It looked like the story of the century was in the making.

The question at this point was how to get to the cave where the tribe was still supposedly living in the Stone Age. Because of the thick jungle and uneven terrain, it was impossible to cut a strip large enough for even a helicopter to land. Finally it was decided a small party would go in on foot. The group would be headed by the hunter, Dafal, and they would build a makeshift landing pad on top of a 75-foot tree near the Tasadays' cave.

As the helicopters hovered, *National Geographic* representatives and the NBC crew were lowered, along with all of their gear, onto the platform. Then they made their way down the tree. The team was led to the cave to meet those whom "evolutionism" had supposedly left behind. The detachment spent a couple of days filming life in the Stone Age.

The Public Encounters the Age of Stone.

In 1971, the public finally had a chance to meet the naked jungle dwellers of the Stone Age on NBC's *National Geographic* Special, *The Lost Tribes of Mindanao*.

In August of 1972, *National Geographic* gave a spectacular visual presentation of the Tasaday people, along with evolutionary verbiage in an attempt to confirm man's ascent up the tree of evolutionism.

The members of the tribe were naked, except for a slim genital pouch for the men and a grass skirt for the women. The public was told they had no domestic animals, and since they knew nothing of agriculture, they lived off the jungle, dining on roots and grubs. Their tools looked like the oldest tools ever found. Fire was made by whirling a wooden rod back and forth between a man's palms which produced a spark to dried vegetation.

A Prophecy Comes to Light.

Amazingly, the Tasaday remembered a prophecy from their ancestors. They were told that someday an outsider would come and love and protect them and lead them out of darkness. It all seemed so romantic and authentic. The public assumed it must all be true.

Two interpreters were required to communicate. From the *National Geographic* article, we learned that there were 24 members in the tribe and that they, along with their ancestors, had lived in the cave as long as they knew. The article stated the Tasaday seemed to be gentle and affectionate. This is quite contrary to evolutionary thinking, which assumes our early ape-man ancestors were more savage. The day of the headhunters and cannibals is not so long gone that we cannot well remember how cruelly man has treated his neighbor — even within the last few decades. What would the world have been like if evolutionism were true and men had been more "primitive" when they lived hundreds of thousands of years ago?

The Day the Earth Shook.

As a result of evolutionary concern, it was decided that the tribe must be protected from the pollution of outsiders. So a petition was sent to President Marcos requesting that the entire territory become a National Reserve and off-limits to outsiders. Marcos consented, and not another word was heard of the Tasaday people until April 1986 — sending shock waves around the world. The Stone Age tribe had been a fraud, a plot masterminded to swindle both the National Geographic Society and the NBC-TV network. They had been suckered — hook, line and sinker-by the gentle "Tasadays." Dafal, who was a "playboy bureaucrat" more than the "hunter," and his partners had seen an opportunity to make some easy money. But the day of reckoning eventually arrived.

President Marcos Ousted.

It was after President Marcos was overthrown from office in 1986, that a Swiss journalist decided to visit the tribe. However, he found the caves empty and began searching for the missing tribe. It wasn't long before confessions came forth. The Tasaday had been put up to posing as cave-dwellers.

The Rest of the Story.

The name *Tasaday* was concocted and the Stone Age tribe came from a village on the other side of the hill from the cave. The people were farmers who lived in houses and slept in beds. They lived a carefree life and hunted more for fun than for necessity. They wore clothes like anyone else — even Levi shirts. They had been reluctant to remove their clothes and act like Stone Age people, but for a small fee, they were persuaded to do so, especially for the benefit of the American visitors. They had to practice using the Stone Age tools and the primitive way of making fire. The most difficult part of the act was achieving the "hollow head" stare of the Stone Ager since human intelligence was supposedly just beginning to emerge. The con artists kept pathways and villages concealed. Even the interpreters were in on the swindle. The prophetic oracle was added to provide a special mystical significance to the entire production.

How Did the American Press Miss It?

On April 13, 1986, the European press carried the news of the hoax to every major newspaper throughout Europe. How is it possible that the American newspapers somehow missed such a major piece of news? Maybe the phone lines were down between Europe and America at that time, or perhaps the operators were on coffee break. The only TV network that gave any exposure of the swindle was NBC's competitor, CBS, on their program *60 Minutes*. It must be quite embarrassing for such a prestigious society as National Geographic to have succumbed to such an outlandish hoax. One would think that a professional organization would admit its folly and make a full confession to its readers. However, that is merely a wishful thought; the public was left with the lie in their minds. Because the American media is so committed to evolutionism, it did not find it necessary to report this incredible counter-evidence to the public. Furthermore, the American liberal media is a close-knit operation, and its members generally seek to cover for one another.

More than two years later *National Geographic*

finally attempted to defend its position. In the September 1988 issue, on page 304, we read a one line response to the find: "Recent stories that the Tasaday were a hoax have been largely discredited."

Such an attitude reveals how unwilling a rebellious man's heart is to surrender to the truth. Since the hoax was revealed, it has been fully documented in detail. *Time/Life Publishers* covers the entire spectacle in one of its series entitled, *Hoaxes and Deceptions*. In it we read, "Hardly anyone now credits that the Tasaday were a reality except a small minority of scientists."[33]

Who is this Small Minority of Scientists?

In 1993, *Nova* produced an hour-long documentary — *The Lost Tribe,* for PBS-TV. The program attempted to unlock the mystery of the lost tribe by interviewing scholars who investigated the allegations. Those who had nothing to gain or lose presented the truth: that all the evidence leads to a cunning case of fraud. However, those (small minority of scientists) who had much to lose had a different perspective. Their faith had not been daunted in the least. According to them, the Tasaday tribe was genuine — in spite of all the evidence to the contrary.

It is obvious how NBC was duped. The humanistic media is anxious to seek out sensational subject matter to maintain its ratings. On the other hand, *National Geographic* is supposed to be a respectable society. It was duped because of its preconceived ideas. It very much wanted it to be true.

Chapter Thirty-One

A Medley of Evolutionary Deceptions

The Margaret Mead Menace.

The Tasaday affair is not the first occasion in which the West has been taken in by the East. The Margaret Mead story is a classic case of a young researcher with a preconceived idea who went to search for evidence. Of course, she found it. Her preconception was that the Judeo-Christian ethic imposed upon adolescents' discovery of sexuality conflicted with nature's natural biological rhythms of life. Miss Mead went to Samoa which at the time was a culture essentially free from the Judeo-Christian influence. She began to question a small group of teenage girls, who quickly caught on to what the American visitor wanted to hear.

They told the 23-year-old Mead the most farfetched stories of a happy society with "free love under the palm trees." None of it was true. The "research" was an instant success among those who wanted scientific license for immorality. As a result, the moral standards of North American life have steadily declined. Mead published her work in 1926. The truth was not disclosed until some 50 years later.

Deception always follows preconceived ideas. The sensational stories, such as the one about Tasaday people or Mead's findings in Samoa, are presented to the public with great fanfare. Years later, the truth finally emerged: It was all a misinterpretation or even an outright hoax. But very rarely does this become news, and the public is left with the lie. When examined closely, the entire evolutionary edifice is built upon this type of imaginary evidence which has been forcefully planted in the public mind. Man will continue to be deceived and taken for a wild ride if he refuses to believe the truth.

Krao Farini: Another Missing Link.

This case was about a rare condition of abnormal hair development over the whole body **(see figs. #75A and B)**. One girl with this condition, Krao Farini, was born in Burma. At about six years of age, she was exhibited at the Royal Aquarium in London, in 1882. Newspapers gave the opinion that this was a case of atavism, or reversion to a low ape-like ancestor. The popular *Scientific American* for 1883 promoted this view by quoting from a German correspondent. The widely circulated *English Mechanic,* reporting in 1894, was more forthright, and titled their article *Krao Farini: The Missing Link.*

The general public had little choice but to believe that some kind of living "missing link" had been discovered in the jungles of Burma. In 1883, the truth of the matter was reported in the more obscure pages of the *British Medical Journal*, where it was pointed out that it was simply a rare case of Hypertrichosis Universalis. Far from having lived a wild life in the jungles, Krao's mother was actually employed at the court of the king of Laow, while Krao herself was a very intelligent child who became fluent in English, French and German.

Children Born with a "Tail."

This is a favorite piece of evolutionary "evidence" which seems to resurface in the press every decade or so. The most recent article was reported in May 1982 in North American newspapers. The article was titled, *Child Born with a Tail*. But the facts were more objectively reported in the *New England Journal of Medicine*

Figure #75A. A RARE GENETIC MISCUE

Figure #75B.

in which the medical profession was careful to point out that the phenomenon is not a tail and contains no bones, but is fatty tissue known as a caudal appendage. Nevertheless, the press still prefers to leave the impression that an evolutionary throwback has occurred.

These few examples regarding media bias relate to the origin of man, but there are many other examples from other fields in which the media has uncritically accepted the word of the scientist and deceived the public. It should be quickly added that not all scientists are deceived. Usually only those with a particular commitment to a preconceived notion: that man has evolved rather than was created. Many times they in turn deceive others unintentionally, yet convincingly. The overall effect has reinforced the evolutionary thought of the ascent of man from brutal beginnings. Unfortunately, many Christians have uncritically accepted from television and popular sophisticated magazines the lies upon which the evolutionary ascent of man is supported.

Chapter Thirty-Two

Escape from Reason

Apes, Men or Frauds.

All fossils which have been found are either 100% ape, 100% men — or 100% fraud. Absolutely no in-between creatures have been found. This has become so painfully obvious that even the evolutionists are reporting more and more about the lack of evidence that surrounds the issue of the transitional form — the missing link.

Lack of Evidence.

For example, here is a cover page article from the weekly science section of *The Dallas Morning News,* titled "Conflicting Evidence Muddies Path For Scientists Tracking Human Origins":

> Because of the lack of evidence, controversy surrounds just about every step of human evolution, from Lucy's

first footfalls to the Neanderthals' last gasp about 35,000 years ago.

Instead of a well-defined theory, human evolution has a handful of fossils and a pile of contradictory genetic and archaeological evidence about the human past.[34]

Major News Magazines State the Facts.

The writer of an article on the origin of man candidly writes:

> Still, doubts about the secrets about man's emergence remain. Scientists concede that their most cherished theories are based on embarrassingly few fossil fragments and that huge gaps exist in the fossil record.[35]

Listen to this statement in *Discover,* science magazine's cover story regarding one of the most recent fossil discoveries:

> "We no longer know who gave rise to whom, perhaps not even how or when we came into being. No better argument can be made to support the time trouble, and cost of field work than this new skull. Like an earthquake, the new

> skull has reduced our nicely organized constructions (*ape-men charts*) to a rubble of awkward, sharp-edged new hypothesis. It's a sure sign of scientific progress.[36]

If it is progress to go back to zero, then we have a new definition of progress! In other words, they don't have a clue as to who begat whom. As Richard Leakey pointed out to his colleagues after he found Skull 1470:

> Either we toss out this skull or we toss out our theories of early man.[37]

His reason for making the statement was that his supposedly 2.8-million-year-old skull is more human looking than those creatures that are theorized on the evolutionary charts to be leading up to man. In other words, Mr. Leakey was asking how the grandson (Skull 1470) could be older than the grandpa? The other so-called "missing links" on the charts were supposedly younger than Skull 1470, but were more apelike. This is why the article concluded with:

> "This skull leaves in ruins the notion that all early fossils can be arranged in an orderly sequence of evolutionary change.[38]

A New Theory.

As a result of the total confusion and the lack of evidence regarding the missing links (the whole chain!) evolutionists are escaping to new realms of absurdity. Their new fantasy is called "punctuated equilibrium," and its tale is carried in *Newsweek* magazine.[39] Simply stated, it says that there are no missing links because there never were any links between ape and man. "Instead of changing gradually as one generation shades into the next, evolution as Gould (a prominent evolutionist) sees it proceeds into discrete leaps. According to the theory of punctuated equilibrium, there are no transitional forms, between species and thus no missing links."

Before they came up with this theory, evolutionists claimed that the reason for the difficulty in finding missing links was that evolutionism happened so slowly, we couldn't see the changes happening, and it was difficult to find any fossil ape-men because changes were just too gradual.

This new theory claims that evolution happens so fast (in sudden leaps) that we shall never find any evidence. One species changes instantly and suddenly into another. Now do you understand the significance of the title of this volume, *The ABCs of Evolutionism: Ape-Man, Batman, Catwomen and Other Evolutionary Fantasies?*

PART VII
BIGFOOT AND OTHER ABOMINABLE CREATURES

Chapter 33: Bigfoot: Fact or Fantasy?
Chapter 34: Outcasts of Job's Day
Chapter 35: Bigfoot of the Bible
Chapter 36: Twenty-first Century Cavemen

Chapter Thirty-Three

Bigfoot: Fact or Fantasy?

(See fig. #76.)
Bugs Bunny or Bigfoot?

With all of the extraterrestrial creatures coming out of Hollywood these days, they are becoming more widely accepted as reality than fiction by the public. As a result, many are reporting they have seen strange creatures in their homes, backyards, on camping trips, etc. Claims range anywhere from Bugs Bunny and Yosemite Sam to monsters, ghosts, demons and other paranormal creatures. They include Bigfoot and other so-called "missing links." Most of these reports are nothing more than the product of imaginations running wild after watching extraterrestrial horror movies while eating junk food. However, there may be truth to some of the sightings of the strange and bizarre creatures known as Bigfoot.

Figure #76. BIGFOOT: FACT OR FANTASY?

What is the Truth About Bigfoot?

Today from remote areas of the Earth come eyewitness reports of creatures that may be animal forms or degenerate humans. Some believe these creatures are humans who have an isolation complex. They have been described as leading isolated lives much like that of an animal. These creatures wear no clothing, and their body hair is reported to be long. They are described as being massive in size, which could be the result of a pituitary gland malfunction. Some have been reported to be over eight feet tall and weighing about 600 pounds. Accounts state that they look and live like animals, but they seem to be human.

Acromegaly.

A disorder of the pituitary gland known as acromegaly can cause giantism. Alton the Giant lived in Chicago during the early part of this century. He was eight-and-a-half feet tall and wore shoes 26 inches long. He suffered from acromegaly. A Frenchman named Maurice Tillet also suffered from this gland disorder; in his case it caused him to appear brutish. Although he was a college graduate, his ferocious appearance led him to become a wrestler. At one point, he was attired like a primitive Neanderthal man and placed among other life-sized Neanderthals in the Field Museum of Natural History in Chicago. Both Maurice and Alton did not live long.

In the mountains of the western United States, there is supposedly a creature known as Bigfoot. In Canada it is called Sasquatch. In Asia they are called Yetis or Abominable Snowmen, and in East Africa they are called Thechebo. These creatures have been sighted both in the past and in the present in various places around the world.

What is the Evidence?

In the last decade there have been over 300 documented sightings of the illusive Bigfoot roaming the northwest United States. With so many sightings, there may be some truth to stories about this hairy fellow. There have always been legendary creatures, some of which have only recently become known.

Recent Discoveries of Living Fossils.

It is interesting to note that there are creatures living today that only have recently been discovered. There is the gorilla, the Komodo dragon, and even the panda bear of China, which wasn't discovered by westerners until 1937. New species are being discovered every year. Many creatures of the past have survived — the alligator, for instance. According to the evolutionary timetable, it is a leftover remnant from the days of the dinosaur. The coelacanth fish **(see fig. #77)**, which evolutionists believed had been extinct for 65 million years, was discovered in 1938 off the east coast of Africa. It had been reported that the

Figure #77. A LIVING FOSSIL

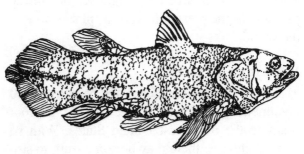

Claimed to be extinct for 65 million years by the evolutionists, the coelacanth (a six-foot fish) was found eaten by the natives of East Africa. If this creature has been alive all along, the question remains: how many other theories and evolutionary dates are also erroneous?

natives were eating this fish for dinner.

Evolutionary Cover-up

The evolutionary community does not want to admit such creatures exist because it would discredit their theory that they existed only millions of years ago.

Many creatures living today do not fit well within the context of evolutionism. For our purposes, the issue really isn't whether or not such creatures do or do not presently exist, but what are they if they do exist? The Bible gives some clues regarding the validity of their existence. In fact, for an accurate approach to the anthropological study of ancient man, one must turn to the Bible.

Chapter Thirty-Four

Outcasts of Job's Day

The Cavemen of Job's Day.

Job lived not long after Noah's Flood. In the book of Job, there are two references to wild humans. They had become wild outcasts because people had oppressed and persecuted them. There are numerous reasons why people oppress others. History reveals that people often oppress others because they are different, particularly, if their appearance is grotesque or their behavior demonic. Could this be the case in Job's day?

> But now they mock me, men younger than I, whose fathers I would have disdained to put with my sheep dogs. Of what use was the strength of their hands to me, since their vigor had gone from them? Haggard from want and hunger, they roamed the parched land in desolate wastelands at night. In the

brush they gathered salt herbs, and their food was the root of the broom tree. They were banished from their fellow men, shouted at as if they were thieves. They were forced to live in the dry stream beds, among the rocks and in holes in the ground. They brayed among the bushes and huddled in the undergrowth (Job 30:1-7).

They thrust the needy from the path and force all the poor of the land into hiding. Like wild donkeys in the desert, the poor go about their labor of foraging food; the wasteland provides food for their children. They gather fodder in the fields and glean in the vineyards of the wicked. Lacking clothes, they spend the night naked; they have nothing to cover themselves in the cold (Job 24:4-7).

Here we have a picture of people who brayed like animals, ate roots and berries from the bushes, and lived in caves. There are people in remote areas of the world today who do the same. Some of these degenerate (morally, spiritually, genetically and physically) folk may have become wild creatures such as Bigfoot, Sasquatch or Yeti, the Abominable Snowman. They eat like animals and scrounge for food. They live in caves and among the rocks. They eat grass and beetles. They have no constructed shelter. They are naked.

The poor souls mentioned in the book of Job were outcasts of their day. Some of them may have developed even a pituitary condition, which could have added to their already grotesque appearance: things such as abnormal body hair, additional height, bone thickening and other physical deformities. This would have isolated them from the rest of society. The book, *Human Oddities* by Martin Monestier, mentioned previously, documents such unbelievable and unsightly physical conditions that have afflicted the human species throughout history.

Chapter Thirty-Five

Bigfoot of the Bible

Sin Leads to Insanity.

The conditions of insanity which have occurred in man throughout history can be caused by a genetic defect or a chemical imbalance in the brain. The Bible also informs us that madness can come from demonic harassment or possession.

From time to time, King Saul was harassed by an evil spirit. The Bible teaches that sin in a person's life can lead to demonic control and savage behavior. Sin is insanity. Sin is deliberately turning out the light and walking in darkness. When a person chooses to live in sin and rebellion, the door is open for him to become demonically controlled and/or possessed. We find this to be the case in the life of a king in the book of Daniel.

Hair as Long as Feathers.

> You will be driven away from people and will live with the wild animals; you will eat grass like cattle. Seven times will pass by for you until you acknowledge that the Most High is sovereign over the kingdoms of men and gives them to anyone he wishes (Dan. 4:32,33).

These words spoken about King Nebuchadnezzar of Babylon, were fulfilled immediately. He was driven away from people and ate grass like cattle. His body was drenched with the dew of heaven until his hair grew long like the feathers of an eagle and his nails grew long like the claws of a bird.

King Nebuchadnezzar was punished by God because of his pride. He ate, lived and thought as an animal. **(See fig. #76.)** Then, after some years, his mind was restored and he became normal again.

Here we have an unusual story in Scripture of a human who became like and lived as an animal. Nebuchadnezzar apparently had some genetic imbalance that caused the hair on his body to grow like that of an animal. His nails became like bird's claws, suggesting that they were somewhat twisted in appearance. Nebuchadnezzar was an example of a creature somewhat like the Bigfoot of the northwestern United States. Thus the "cave people" of both the past and present can be the result of degenerate people, who can be found in the midst of civilization.

From time to time, the media reports on people today who are living in primitive conditions. For example, one day I picked up our local newspaper and there was a story about naked cavemen and women living a Stone Age existence in the snowy Himalayas. They were eating raw food because they had not discovered fire.[40]

There are other passages in scripture besides the one about Nebuchadnezzar which mentions people living in caves. David, for instance, lived in a cave for some time after fleeing from King Saul (I Sam. 22:1). At one point, David even pretended to be mad in order to protect himself while he was living among his enemies. To feign madness, he foamed at the mouth. This suggests that people of that time were aware that this happened with some who had mental and physical imbalances (I Sam. 21:13). Another Bible character was a "caveman" for a time. Lot lived in a cave after he fled from the destruction of his home in Sodom (Gen. 19:30).

Living in caves is nothing new. Throughout the ages some have chosen to live in caves for one reason or another. Just because human bones are found in a cave doesn't mean they are the remains of a "missing link." There will always be people — past, present and future — who choose to live in caves.

Chapter Thirty-Six

Twenty-First Century Cavemen

(See fig. #78.)
Definition of a Caveman.

What were the cavemen? They were nothing more than men living in caves. What is a cavewoman? She is nothing more than a woman who has chosen to live in a cave. Get the picture? Cave people are people who have chosen to live in a cave.

Neanderthal people, the Cro-Magnon people and other so-called cave people, were the descendants of Noah and his family. After the Tower of Babel incident, mankind split into groups and began migrating to different parts of the world. Once the people became isolated, they sought shelter in caves during the cold winter months. Thus, they became known as cavemen. Even today there are cave people in various parts of the world. Some of these live by

Figure #78. TWENTY-FIRST CENTURY CAVEMEN

POPULAR VIEW OF MAN'S ORIGIN

hunting, using spears, tools made of stone or bone, and bows and arrows.

Petra: Capital of the Ancient Edomites.

Petra is an ancient city in southwest Jordan. It is carved out of gigantic cliffs of solid stratified rock. It seems incredible that an entire civilization dwelled entirely in a city built in caves. More than 1,000 years before Christ, the people of Petra were highly civilized and were involved in extensive trading with the nations of the world.

Modern Cave People.

There are other cave people who are quite civilized and educated. I once visited a large population of gypsies who live in the caves of Grenada, located in southern Spain. The caves were fully furnished — complete with electricity and plumbing. The walls were decorated, and many of the cave homes had multiple bedrooms. The gypsies lived in them because they were cool during the hot summers and the rent was cheap.

I also visited a large population of people living in caves in eastern Turkey. These caves were originally lived in by the first and second century Christians who fled persecution from the Romans. I have walked through numerous catacombs beneath the city of Rome where it was said that tens of thousands of Christians lived and died at the height of Roman persecution.

Hip Cave Dwellers.

Today, it is a well-known fact that many American youth have dropped out of society and left their parent's comfortable homes to live a life free from moral restraints. They live in caves or in tropical places such as Hawaii, where they wear little or nothing and engage in free sex. They live off the land. There is little need of physical protection. They live a very simple lifestyle. They have little to do with the outside world. During the 1960s and 70s, during the height of the hippie movement, countries like Afghanistan were hotspots which attracted American societal dropouts by the thousands because hallucinogenic and other illegal drugs were easily accessible and cheap. The Bible speaks clearly about this kind of lifestyle, which is often the result of a morally decadent heart.

Cave People Shall Always be Around.

There are not contradictions between God's Word and science as some would believe. Cave people have existed all through history. They probably will always be around. They aren't new. After they die, eventually their bones will be found.

On the other hand, the contradictions between the fantasy of evolutionism and the facts regarding ape-men will continue to persist as long as there are people who reject God's Word and His will for their lives. Some become so degenerate they behave like the one mentioned in the following Scripture:

> When Jesus got out of the boat, a man with an evil spirit came from the tombs to meet him. This man lived in the tombs, and no one could bind him any more, not even with a chain. For he had often been chained hand and foot, but he tore the chains apart and broke the irons on his feet. No one was strong enough to subdue him. Night and day among the tombs and in the hills he would cry out and cut himself with stones (Mk. 5:2-5).

Luke reports that he ran around naked (Lk. 8:27). For a long time this man had not worn clothes or lived in a house, but had lived in the tombs. He was delivered by the power of Jesus.

Science rejects Bigfoot because his existence is based primarily on oral testimony. Although there have been a number of photographs taken of the creature, the quality of each photograph has generally been very poor. Other evidences have come forth such as a tape recording of the sounds which the creature supposedly made and samples of hair collected. Even the U.S. Army has given the fellow recognition by providing a map giving locations where the creature has been sighted. One town has reported ten sightings, and the citizens who saw him were given polygraph tests to confirm their stories. The point is that cavemen have always been and always will be around. Just because a person lives in a cave for whatever reason doesn't mean he is half-man and half-beast. Thus cavemen are a weak link to the theory of evolutionism and not a missing link. For an accurate approach to the anthropological study of ancient man, one must turn to the Bible.

PART VIII
THE MAKING OF MAN

Chapter 37: Stone Age Mating Game: Comparative Anatomy

Chapter 38: Kinks in the Links

Chapter 39: The Marks of Man

Chapter 40: The Impassable Gap

Chapter Thirty-Seven

Stone Age Mating Game: Comparative Anatomy

(See fig. #79.)
There is Still More ...

With the overwhelming evidence being against evolutionists' wildest dreams of apes becoming man, it would be of value to consider several additional issues that will add insult to injury to the ridiculous notion that simians sired sapiens. By examining the anatomy of the apes and comparing them it becomes obvious that some time in the distant past there must have been a Stone Age mating game.

Bridging the Gap.

Evolutionists determine the similarities between man and ape by looking at their bones. They claim that the similarities between humans and apes prove they are descendants of one another.

Stone Age Mating Game: Comparative Anatomy

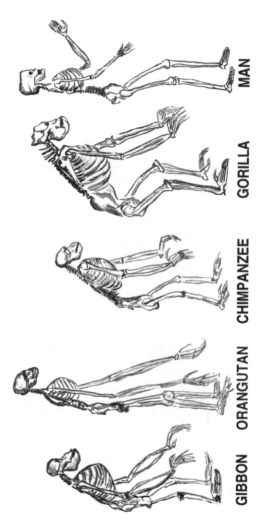

Figure #79. COMPARATIVE ANATOMY: A LOOK AT APES AND MAN

However, watching evolutionary attempts at selecting man's ancestor from the ape family has been like watching a three-ring circus. In some respects the gorilla resembles man, but its skull is more like a chicken's because it has a bony crest **(see fig. #80)**; man's skull is smooth. (Fortunately, no one has suggested that the chicken

Figure #80. LINKING CHICKENS TO CHIMPANZEES

and ape sired the first human!) Man has 12 pairs of ribs and the gorilla has 13. Although the gibbon has 12 pairs of ribs and a stomach most like a man's stomach, it has arms which reach down below its ankles. The chimpanzee has shorter arms but has 13 pairs of ribs. Did Mother Nature take one pair from its side to make man? Of all the ape's the shape of the orangutan's brain is closest to man's, but its feet have thumbs for big toes. All apes and baboons have this anatomical feature, so they, in effect, have four hands. **(See fig. #81.)** Apes are gorilla-walking quadrupeds. **(See fig. #82.)** The only resemblance a baboon has to man is its spine.

All in the Family Powwow.

Hollywood has produced some ridiculous and hilarious movies regarding the evolutionary concept about the emergence of prehistoric man. However, no one has yet produced a movie suggesting that the family of apes had a big pow wow where they sired man. This idea is absurd. But since there are some similarities between man and the ape family, it isn't any more bizarre than what evolutionists have proposed. There is not one kind of ape with which man has any special or exclusive similarity. **(See figs. #83A and B.)**

Evolutionists assume that man originated from the ape family, and since even they find it difficult to believe that man evolved from any kind of ape that exists today, they assume it is some creature from the remote past. Since such

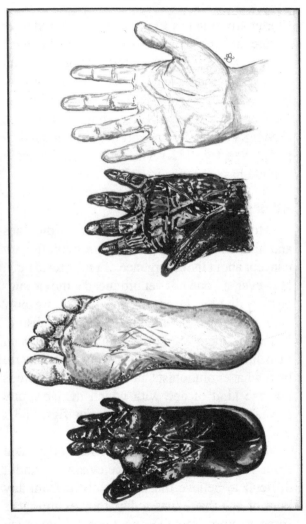

Figure #81. FOUR HANDS OR FOUR FEET?

Figure #82. QUADRUPEDS: FOUR ON THE FLOOR

a fellow has not been identified yet, they suggest this illusive creature has become extinct. This sounds like good science fiction, but not good science.

Not Even Close.

There is an obvious difference between the skulls of humans and apes. The brain case of the

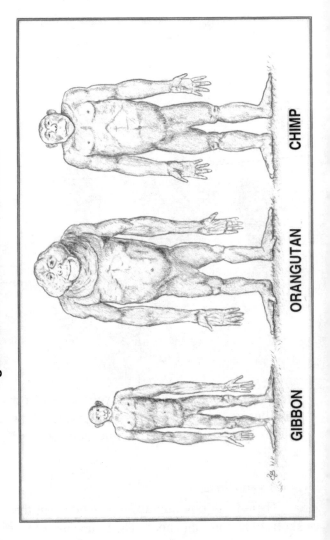

Figure #83A. LOOKING AT THE LINEUP

Stone Age Mating Game: Comparative Anatomy

Figure #83B.

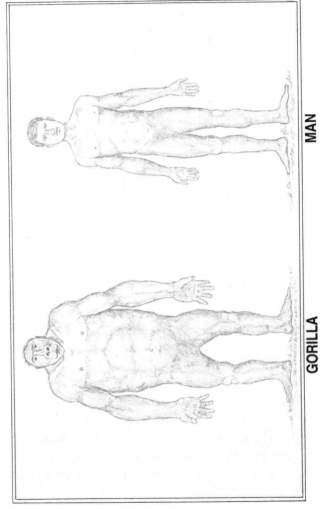

human skull is two-thirds of the head's mass. The face takes up one-third. It is the reverse in the apes; the face is large and the brain is small. **(See fig. #84.)**

Overall Skeletal Similarities.

To say that men and baboons are closely related because they both have ribs is like saying that a butterfly and the U.S. Space Shuttle are closely related because they both have wings. **(See fig. #85.)** It is foolishness to use similarities to prove a relationship. It is even more foolish to think that bones alone make the difference between animals and humans.

As previously mentioned, the buzz word which has replaced "missing link" is "ancient common ancestor." The concept of an "ancient common ancestor" has arisen out of necessity; there is absolutely no evidence for previous theories. This "ancient common ancestor" supposedly existed in Earth's distant past and fathered both apes and humans. This is a convenient theory which draws attention away from the glaring truth that the missing links are still missing, and that in fact, they never existed in the first place.

Stone Age Mating Game: Comparative Anatomy

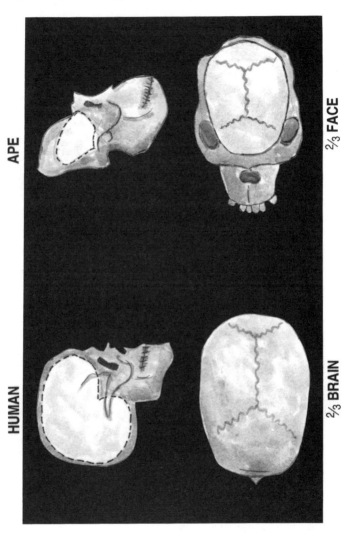

Figure #84. SIZING UP THE BRAINS

Figure #85. THEY MUST BE RELATIVES

BOTH HAVE WINGS

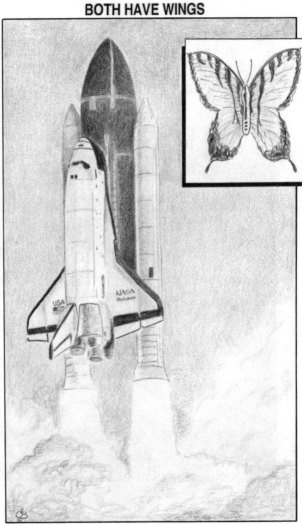

What Makes Man Different from the Ape?

It is as impossible for man to have come from an ape as it would be for an ape to come from applesauce. What makes man special isn't his bones, but that he was made in the image of his Creator.

The mental and moral chasm separating man from animal is wider than the expanse of the universe. Even the pagan philosopher, Aristotle, acknowledged this. Men, no matter how savage, have always instinctively recognized that their existence is different and superior to the entire animal creation. This is due to the spiritual nature created after God's image that He put within man. Evolutionists attempt to bridge the gap between ape and man with their mythological fantasy: "Once upon a time an ape-man woke up and realized he was no longer a simian but a homo sapien." This kind of deception is not new to man; it was revealed long ago in the Bible (Rom. 2). The farther man removes himself from God, the more darkened his mind becomes. He conjures silly and ridiculous tales, such as the ABCs of evolutionism, instead of believing the truth.

"Man Became a Living Soul" (Gen. 2:7 KJV).

The Hebrew word for *soul* cannot mean monkey material. God didn't take pre-existing material when He breathed into man the breath of life. The context means that God used inorganic material and created Adam in an instant, not over millions of years from apes.

Chapter Thirty-Eight

Kinks in the Links

Bones of Contention.

Not only does the evolutionary ape-man theory lack evidence from fossils, it contains many kinks. Attempts to resolve these conflicts require absurd mental gymnastics.

Kink One: Snap, Crackle and Pop.

How did the ape-men survive for millions of years in the very uncomfortable half-bent position? Apes walk on all fours; man is the only mammal who walks on two feet. No skeletal fossil has been found of a creature in a half-bent posture.

Nevertheless, if these unfortunate mortals did exist, at some point they were transformed into fully-erect individuals as suggested in the movie, *Caveman,* staring Ringo Star, the famous Beatles' drummer in the 60s. The "Neanderthals" in the film were depicted hunched over, shuffling along in a contorted way throughout half the movie. During one scene, there was a reunion between one of the elderly members of the clan who had been separated and lost from the rest of the tribe for a time. Upon reuniting, there was a robust display of affection. One embrace was so intense, the bones of the elderly ape-man began snapping, crackling and popping. Suddenly, a pleasant smile appeared on the elderly ape-man's face as he realized his present state of comfort was because he was standing in a fully erect position.

The other ape-men quickly followed suit. There was a sudden outburst of affectionate hugs among the "Neanderthals." After a furor of snapping and crackling bones, the entire tribe began grunting pleasantries to one another because they were able to stand and walk erectly. They no longer had to shuffle along bowlegged and hunched over.

Maybe evolutionists obtained this idea from visiting chiropractors. They squeeze their patients to pop their bones back into place to relieve discomfort. This theory makes about as much sense as other theories postulated by the evolutionary community.

Kink Two: Big Toe Baloney.

How could the foot of an ape with its four toes and a thumb gradually evolve into man's 5-toe foot. Apes use their big toes mainly for gripping as they swing in the trees. The thumbs on the ape's feet have a separate muscle. However, a human's big toe is bound together by one muscle and does not have a strong grip. **(See fig. #86.)** How could apes slowly evolving toward man be able to keep their grip high in the treetops? Losing their grip would be disastrous, and bring the whole process of evolution to an end. No fossils of a creature with an intermediate big toe have ever been found. Every skeleton found has clearly revealed the big toe is either 100% ape or 100% man.

Kink Three: IQ Hike.

How would an ape gradually become more intelligent? There is no evidence of any creature throughout recorded history becoming more intelligent. Fossil records reveal that in ancient times, all creatures were much larger than they are today. If intelligence is measured by brain size, then modern apes are less intelligent than prehistoric apes, which had larger skulls.

Likewise, some of the so-called prehistoric men, such as the Cro-Magnon man, had bigger

Figure #86. BIG TOE BALONEY

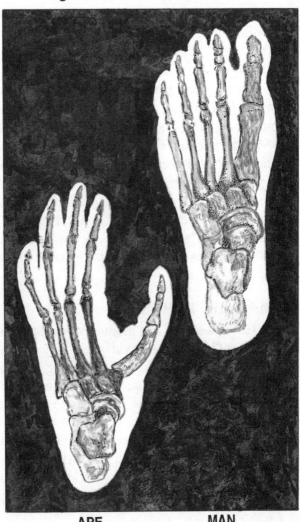

APE　　　　MAN

brains than most human adults today. Furthermore, a human's brain is smaller than a whale's or an elephant's. The ratio of brain weight to body weight is more in a sparrow than in a man.

Man: 2.5% of total body weight

Sparrow: 4.2% of total body weight

Sparrows are not more intelligent than man. The power of man's mind is infinitely different than any of the creature's — including the ape's. Volume 11 of the Creation Series will explain how man's intelligence today is but a fraction of that of his early ancestors'. Original man was far superior in every way to man of the 21st century.

Kink Four: A Tale of a Monkey.

If the ancestors of all monkeys and apes had tails, how and why did some lose them and others did not? Did the styles change? Was it no longer fashionable to wear a tail? After all, intelligence was on the rise, making such options a real possibility.

Kink Five: Mother Nature's Beauty Salon.

Why and when did man lose his body hair which never needed cutting? Why did he acquire head hair, which needs cutting? The reverse is true in the ape family. From a biblical perspective, the answer is obvious.

God provided apes and monkeys with short body hair which doesn't need cutting because He knew they could never make tools. Long hair would be a disadvantage in the trees. Remember Absalom? He was killed because his long hair got hung up in a tree (II Sam. 18:9).

Monkeys would never have the skill to make clothes. The apes' body hair made it possible for the babies to cling to their mother's hair while moving through the trees. On the other hand, humans were given the intelligence to care for their hair and body and to make clothes to cover themselves.

Evolutionists have a problem when it comes to illustrating ape-women. They don't have a clue as to when their head hair began to grow long. They don't want to give them a crew cut because they will look too much like an ape. Long hair would make them look too feminine. So Mrs. Pitifulcus ape-woman has a short 1920s bobbed hairdo with a 1990s weather-blown look, somewhat frizzed. **(See figs. #87A-C.)**

Why do men of science struggle with such ridiculous arguments? The answer is found in the words of Solomon. He stated that if a man begins with a foolish foundation, his dream house will look like a monstrosity (Eccl. 10:13). The ABCs of evolutionism are built on that kind of foundation.

Figure #87A. MISS PITIFULCUS: ONLY HER HAIRDRESSER KNOWS

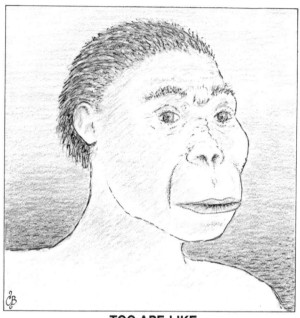

TOO APE-LIKE

Figure #87B.

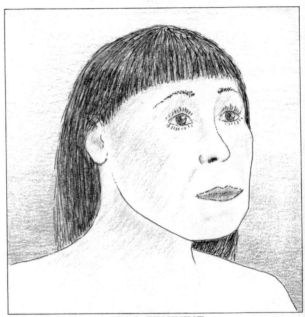

TOO FEMININE

Figure #87C.

JUST RIGHT

Chapter Thirty-Nine

The Marks of Man

Five Unique Distinctions.

There is an infinite chasm between an ape and a human. A human can split atoms, paint the ceiling of the Sistine Chapel, compose the *Hallelujah Chorus*, send a man to the moon, and perform delicate heart surgery. The abyss that separates the smartest ape from the dullest human is vast. There are a host of things separating man from the ape family. We shall consider five distinctions which mark the uniqueness of man. **(See fig. #88.)**

1. Tools

What makes a tool, a tool? A tool implies that there was a toolmaker. Just because some bones of knuckle-walking apes have been found along with some crude tools is no sign the apes were evolving. Even modern apes use "tools" (if we can call them that). They can be seen using a

Figure #88. THE MARKS OF MAN

fractured piece of flint rock as a cutting tool. Actually, all that an ape does is select a rock that will fit in his hand for a particular use.

Chimpanzees sometimes use small sticks to dig grub from a hole. But this is a zillion miles from tribesmen who make bows and arrows, stone knives and blow guns, to shoot down monkeys and birds from the treetops of the rain forest.

If examples of apes using implements in any way suggests they are on their way to becoming man or have become man, then maybe we should write our congressmen in Washington to consider the words of the famous evolutionary authoropoligist, Dr. Louis Leakey:

> Either we're going to have to change our definition of man, or invite the chimps to send a representative to the United Nations.[41]

In other words, the tools of man, no matter how primitive they may seem to us, are very advanced compared to the stick or piece of rock used by a chimp. A monkey is not on its way to becoming man just because it drags a branch from time to time.

2. Fire

Animals instinctively know the danger that can come from fire. The heat immediately signals them of potential danger. No one has ever witnessed *any* kind of animal using fire in *any* way, let alone having command of it.

3. Art

Although there is beauty in the numerous types of nests constructed by birds, it is there because each bird has been programmed to repeat the distinctive design of the previous generation of birds. They do not add nor significantly deviate from the pattern.

This same thing can be seen throughout nature with any creature constructing a habitat for its family. No creature has ever produced a work of art even as simple as my son's paintings in his preschool days **(see fig. #89)**, let alone a masterpiece created by such illustrious celebrated artists as Picasso, Leonardo da Vinci, van Gogh or Michelangelo — to name a few.

4. Speech

We have read about chimpanzees that supposedly demonstrate language is not restricted to humans after all. However, this is mere wishful thinking. Psycholinguists (those who study psy-

Figure #89. ANY ART AIN'T APE-MAN ART

chological and the mental processes involved in language) point out that there are 16 unique design features of speech and language. These 16 features are outlined in the book by Dr. Clifford

Wilson entitled, *Monkeys Will Never Talk.* Only humans have all 16. Chimps have several. So do dolphins, dogs, cats and other living creatures.

Even the voice apparatus of humans is uniquely designed for the fantastic processes needed to create sentences. There are tribesmen alive today who are uncivilized in many ways. However, their ability to speak, imitate the sounds of birds perfectly, and describe creatures only from their imprints in sand, reveal their remarkable intelligence.

Just because a trainer can teach an ape to make a so-called conversational grunt by hanging a banana in front of him, doesn't mean that's conversation. The difference between that and the conversation of a five-year-old child is like that of night to day. Even if a trainer could get 1,000 different kinds of grunts or actions from a trained ape, that would still be a long way from human conversation. All the bananas in the world cannot make an ape speak as a human does.

5. Burial

Even the most primitive human beings ever found, either in fossil form or living, have always buried their dead. On the other hand, no ape or baboon has ever been found to do this. There are two primary reasons for burying the dead: valuing life and belief in a future life.

Man makes preparations for a life to come. This is why weapons, useful objects, etc. are often placed in graves. The quality and quantity of burial objects varies tremendously between the highly cultivated civilizations and the primitive cavemen, but all reveal a basic belief in a future life. The altars and images of deities found at ancient sites reveal man's belief in God — or gods. No bird or animal has ever been found making preparations for a life to come or building an altar to God. This is a distinctive mark of man.

Cremation or Burial?

Many evolutionists promote cremation of the dead because they deny God and His promise regarding the resurrection of the dead. They refuse to believe in the biblical perspective of a future life and final judgment. The Bible doesn't say cremation is sin. However, it was not practiced by God's people either in Old or New Testaments' times, though many nations around Israel did burn their dead. In Old Testament days, the Jews buried their dead, with the exception of some criminals, who were burned as punishment. Thus, we learn from Scripture, that burning a body is dishonoring it.

The Jews considered it a tragedy if a person wasn't buried. Both the Hebrews and Christians buried their dead knowing that the cemetery was only a resting place for the body; it would rise again in the resurrection. With all of its frailties, there is a sanctity about the Christian's body. The body is not garbage; each was designed as a house for a person in which to live to fulfill God's purpose. Burial shows respect for the person who was housed in the body. It also shows respect for the body, which is the temple of the Holy Spirit (1 Cor. 6:19). Cremation is disrespectful, especially for those who belong to Christ. A traditional burial says something powerful about the hope of resurrection. Don't let the atheistic evolutionary doctrines of society draw you away from the godly traditions of the Bible. Man is not an animal. Man is a unique creation fashioned after the Creator and has eternal significance.

Conclusion

The above five distinctions between apes and man are but a few on the long list of things that separate them. Why do some people insist that man evolved from apes? When man rejects his Creator, he is left with nothing to guide him in locating his beginnings. As a result, he ends up on a dead-end path that leads to ridiculous and destructive conclusions.

Chapter Forty

The Impassable Gap

The enormous gap between man and ape has never been filled and never will be because the "missing link" does not exist. There is no evidence of worship, music, art, guilt, sympathy, concern for life after death, etc. among apes or in any other form of life besides man. Man is man and ape is ape and never the twain shall meet! To believe otherwise is simply the figment of one's vain imagination. Sometimes we human beings are more stupid than an ox!

> The ox knows his master, the donkey his owner's manger, but Israel does not know, my people do not understand. (Isa. 1:3).

In other words, animals are smart enough to recognize their master, but sometimes we humans, with all our intelligence, don't recognize ours. Many have made nature the one they bow down to and worship. After Adam and Eve left the Garden of Eden, they began to multiply and spread throughout the world. The Garden of Eden, where the Bible states that man was created and originally placed, was located in what anthropologists refer to as the fertile crescent. That is where the oldest remains of civilization have been found.

After the Flood and the Tower of Babel, once again man began to migrate. It didn't take mankind long to move to the ends of the Earth. Early man was apparently quite nomadic. (Today the average American is said to move 16 times during his lifetime.) Early man rapidly dispersed, and soon racial variations began to develop. Some of these groups of people may have eventually become extinct or moved to new locations for ecological reasons. Today, when their bones are found, the racial characteristics are given evolutionary language. The truth of the matter is, they are fully human but have some different physical traits. We see the same kind of differences in racial characteristics today. We also see changes in physical attributes with the passage of time. We have seen many such in the last 50 years.

The Number One Issue

The most important difference between humans and apes is that humans possess a soul. Man has a deep need to worship his Creator. But man cannot know his Creator unless he humbles himself and bows his knee to His Son, Jesus Christ.

> In Him we have redemption through His blood, the forgiveness of sins, in accordance with the riches of God's grace (Eph.1:7).

Only through faith in Christ is there understanding of man's origins as well as of eternal life.

> Salvation is found in no one else, for there is no other name under heaven given to men by which we must be saved (Acts. 4:12).

PART IX
APE-MAN: SPRINGBOARD FOR RACISM

Chapter 41: The Roots of Racism

Chapter 42: New Age Math:
Angle + Slope = IQ?

Chapter 43: Measuring Up to One's Brains

Chapter 44: Sizing Up One's Cerebral Surroundings

Chapter Forty-One

The Roots of Racism

(See fig. #90.)
The Fruit of Evolutionism.

Evolutionism can be found at the very root of atheism, communism, relativism and every other form of anti-Christian practice. Dangerous and deadly social problems are deeply rooted in the purposelessness of materialistic evolutionism: suicide, homosexuality, promiscuity, abortion and chemical abuse — just to name the most obvious. Evolutionism has played a major part in influencing the way humans think of themselves. Problems of low self-esteem, animalistic behavior and depression result from the feeling of meaninglessness in life — that belief in evolution — or lack of belief in God — brings. Evolutionism attacks God's omniscience. If the universe, life and all creatures are comprised of things evolved through chance and error in genetic transmutations, then there is no God. Of all

Figure #90. THE ROOTS AND FRUITS OF EVOLUTIONISM

of the deadly fruit that evolutionism has produced, racism is one of the most toxic. The ABCs of evolutionism breed racism.

One and the Same.

Although the Church hasn't been blameless on the issue of slavery, evolutionism is covered with mud when it comes to racism. What do evolutionism and racism have in common? They both have the same father: Satan. Evolutionism is the breeding ground for racism. However, in these modern and progressive times, evolutionists would never acknowledge that their theory leads to racism. Yet we shall reveal how the ABCs of evolutionism actually breed racism.

One of the chief justifications for racial discrimination in modern times has been the belief that because races allegedly evolved separately, they were at different stages of evolution; therefore, some races were more backward, or simply stated, stupid. Hence, one race was not as fully "human" as another, but rather, something on the level of "Bigfoot" — half-man and half-beast.

The Cause of Racism.

Racism has plagued humanity for thousands of years, and it has especially shown its ugly head during the last few centuries. Think of the myriads of blacks carried from Africa and sold into slavery in the new world and more recently, the blatant racism of the Nazi's of Germany.

To find the causes of racism, we must look at the roots. Of course, sin and selfishness are at the root of racism. The root of all sin is pride. Pride stems from the desire to be God, to take His place as moral governor of the universe. The purpose of evolutionism is to replace God. Evolutionism promotes racism. Its adherents desire to put another down to lift themselves up.

From Darwin on down, evolutionists have preached that the black race was lower on the evolutionary scale — much closer to the apes than Caucasians. The entire concept of race is evolutionary, not biblical. Scripture declares, "From one man he made every nation of men" (Acts 17:26). All of mankind springs from our first parents, Adam and Eve, and then through Noah's family. As previously mentioned, the biblical distinction is between national groups, especially language groups, not skin color nor other physical characteristics. No doubt over the years many blacks have questioned their own self-worth, wondering if their standing before God was equal to that of other ethnic groups.

No Place for Racism in the Bible.

While prejudice, persecution, and racial hatred directly follows evolutionary teaching, some have proposed racism in the name of Christ. The Christian must never entertain such thoughts. Christ certainly didn't. He was likely neither white nor black, but somewhere in-between. He died to provide *all* men the opportunity for eternal life (II Pet. 3:9). Heaven will be populated by "a great multitude ... of all nations, and kindreds, and people, and tongues ... [who will stand] before the throne, and before the Lamb, clothed with white robes ..." (Rev. 7:9 KJV). All people who have repented of sin and turned to follow Christ will be there. In the end, all racism shall be abolished. The truth is, evolutionism has a dark and sinister side. We shall now take a look at how the ape-man fantasy operates as the springboard for racism.

Chapter Forty-Two

New Age Math: Angle + Slope = IQ?

The Angle of the Forehead.

One doesn't have to look very far into evolutionism before blatant signs of racism appear. The evolutionary idea that man is a descendant of the ape insinuates that man's IQ was once the same as an ape. It follows that some ethnic groups have not advanced as much as others have; therefore, intelligence levels differ. Evolutionists, because of their belief that man came from the ape, think that early man's forehead was slanted in an apelike fashion. The evolutionary illustrations of early man reveal their view of his intelligence. In their eyes, the angle of the forehead indicates the level of intelligence.

Evolutionists have concluded that a slanted forehead means an individual is subhuman. The fact is, the angle of the forehead has absolutely nothing to do with intelligence. A high, bulging forehead is no more indicative of intelligence than a receding one. People with skulls shaped like the ancient ones with a low, sloping forehead, can be easily found on the streets of our cities today.

Royal Flatheads.

Human beings vary in appearance for many reasons: racial peculiarities, customs, diseases, gender and age are some of them. Certain uncivilized tribes have had a custom of flattening the heads of the children in their early years. **(See fig. #91.)** The ancient royalty among the Peruvians bound the heads of their newborn babies with boards and wrappings in such a way that their heads were elongated to set apart the Inca rulers from the common people. This custom in no way affected the intelligence of the children. The adult heads of pygmies (about 900 cc.) are much smaller than the average human skull. Some people have high foreheads; some have low and slanting ones. **(See fig. #92.)** These superficial differences in no way indicate either intelligence or lack of it. Believing that man evolved from apes, evolutionists who search for the "missing link" reject skulls with high foreheads and select the low, slanting ones because

Figure #91. ANCIENT INDIAN CUSTOMS

they are more ape-like. Then they assign the skulls an age according to their "ape-likeness." They took skulls of people who died 150 years ago out of the graveyards of Europe. These people lived in a state similar to that of our American Indian. From these skulls only those which served evolutionism's purpose were selected and dubbed ape-men.

Evolutionists come to conclusions regarding

Figure #92. FOREHEADS FOOL SAGES OF SCIENCE

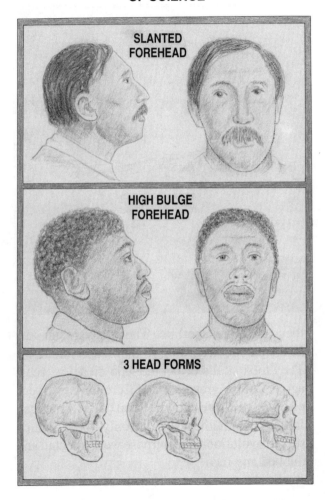

remains based on their living conditions. They assume that the more rudimentary the living conditions, the older the remains. But after Noah's Flood, during the Ice Age or glacial age, men were forced to live in more crude and simplistic conditions than they had earlier. Many lived in caves and existed by the most simple means.

George Washington and the Red Man.

While America's first president, George Washington, was using silver knives and forks for eating and using firearms in war on one part of the American continent, there were Indians using flints and axes made of stone in another part. Even today, while half the world lives in a highly civilized manner, there are people living in a "Stone Age."

They exist in a very crude state. These societies are the remnants of past civilizations that became decadent. The result was judgment, which came either from invading enemies or epidemics, plagues, droughts or some other natural disaster. The survivors must go back seeking out a livelihood often in undeveloped conditions.

It is likely there will always be those on Earth living in primitive conditions. There will always be decadent people. And there probably will always be cave individuals — intelligent people who for one reason or another have chosen to live in caves. So discovering skulls of those who lived in rudimental conditions is no proof at all that they lived millions of years ago or that they were subhuman. Nevertheless, it is easy to see how this evolutionistic view of early man promotes racism.

Chapter Forty-Three

Measuring Up to One's Brains

Another Evolutionary Notion.

Not only have evolutionists taught that the angle of the forehead indicates the level of intelligence, but also that the size of the skull indicates brain capacity and level of intelligence. Small skulls, then, represent less intelligence and are a sign of primitive man. Larger skulls are thought to represent greater intelligence. If that were true, there would be a real problem with the skeletons of the Neanderthals and Cro-Magnon races.

Evolutionists claim that all forms of life evolve from tiny simple forms to larger more complex ones, with the human brain being the most complex. So the evolutionary general trend would have the small to the large, but these ancient skulls reveal the very opposite to be true.

Bigger Brains.

As a matter of fact, many of the fossilized skeletons of what have been named the Neanderthal and Cro-Magnon races were 15% larger and had a greater brain capacity than modern man has.

Who Evolved from Whom?

The evolutionary model holds that increasing brain size is characteristic of human evolution. So, the larger the fossil brain is calculated to be, the more recently evolutionists assume it lived. It is often taught that in the future, man's brain size will evolve to be even larger. This story is popular, but the scientific evidence is against it.

The skull of the first Neanderthal found showed it had a brain capacity of about 1330 cubic centimeters, which is the size of the average male brain in Europe today. There are thousands of people now living who have skulls just like that of Mr. Neanderthal. In fact, with many of the so-called "ancient" skulls, the brain capacity far exceeds that of the average American. For example, the capacity of the La Chapelle-aux-Saints skull found in France is estimated at 1600 cc. Modern man's brain capacity is somewhere between 1200 cc and 1500 cc. **(see fig. #93).**

Figure #93. MODERN MAN HEAD SHRINKERS

BRAIN SIZES OF FOSSIL AND MODERN HUMAN BEINGS

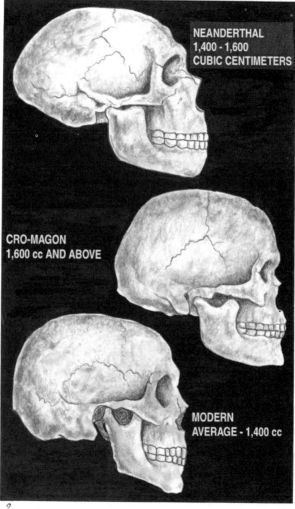

If evolutionism were true, then the Neanderthal-Cro-Magnon fossil race would have a smaller brain size, not a larger one.

If this were true, since the Neanderthal's brain capacity was larger than that of many modern people, the Neanderthals must have evolved from modern man. Or perhaps the human brain size is actually shrinking! A better explanation is that the variation in brain size seen in human fossils is consistent with the variation predicted by genetics and the creation model.

This is explained in the Bible: Before the Flood people lived longer, were healthier and bigger.

Remnants of that original race, which was superior in both size and strength lingered on after the Flood. Today we can still see traces of what man may have been like before the Flood — people with exceptional physical strength, stature, mental capacities or artistic abilities.

Most evolutionists believe that the larger the skull, the more intelligence the person possessed.

A Waste of Brain Space.

In addition to the above evidence, which counters evolutionism, it should be pointed out that evolutionists theorize that bodily organs only evolve if the organism needs to do so in order to survive. Why is it then, that nine-tenths of the brain of modern man is never used, and yet it supposedly evolved anyway?

The fact is that practically all prehistoric animals, birds, insects, plants, trees, etc. were much bigger than their descendants. This Scripture explains that decline in size. It is a result of the curse (Gen. 3) which came upon man and the entire physical world because of man's sin. Little by little, the entire world is perishing. It would eventually end up as a cold cinder in space if it were not for the fact that someday soon the King of the universe will return to Earth and restore nature to its original perfection.

It is obvious that the belief that skull size is directly related to intelligence breeds racism. Therefore, evolutionism is directly responsible for promoting racism.

Chapter Forty-Four

Sizing Up One's Cerebral Surroundings

(See fig. #94.)
A Case of Skulduggery

The term skulduggery carries a negative connotation. It indicates dishonesty. Evolutionists have used every trick in their bag to propagate their atheistic religion. Previously it was pointed out that the skulls of early men were significantly larger than those of modern man. In this chapter we shall explain the various factors contributing to the growth and development of skulls. Today there are a remarkable number of different types of human beings. They differ in size, shape and color, yet they are all living at the same time in Earth history. The notion that the size of skulls is proof for evolutionism is nothing but a myth.

Brain Size Development.

Suppose we found three skulls and named them A, B and C. Each of the three was a different size. The fact that C is the largest skull and A the smallest does not prove that C came after B, and B came after A as man gradually evolved. It could be the opposite. Perhaps B descended from C because he was unable to obtain sufficient and/or nourishing food where he lived; and so was smaller than C. Perhaps B's descendant, A, found it ever harder to find food and thus received even less of the nutrition necessary for proper body development and growth. His skull, therefore, was even smaller. Or it may be that all lived at the same time, only in various regions — some with substantial food sources and others where there was little food to be found.

Taking into consideration environmental factors (such as extremes in weather conditions) and genetic miscues in fetus development, the possibility for variety in size, shape and overall appearance of individuals increases.

Snoopy, Lassie, Benji and Other Furry Mutts.

The great differences that can develop within one kind of animal can also be observed in dogs and cats. But no one considers little dogs to be a

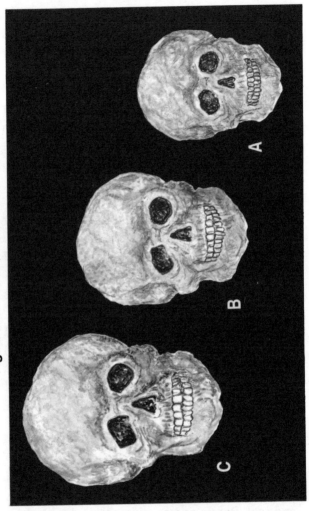

Figure #94. WHO CAME FROM WHOM?

different species from big ones. And certainly no one believes that big dogs evolved from little ones. So why is it that evolutionists think that if a skull is small it must be something other than purely human? There is absolutely no reason to think that a small skull comes from a half-ape/half-man that marks some stage in the gradual development of apes into men.

Caution should be used when associating brain size with intelligence. It is popular to believe that a larger brain size corresponds with greater intelligence. But this assumption is incorrect. Here are several examples:
1. Individual human brain capacities widely vary from 830 cc to 2800 cc in modern peoples *without* a corresponding variation in intelligence.
2. Men average a larger brain capacity than women *without* a corresponding advantage in intelligence.
3. Whales, dolphins and elephants all have larger brains than humans, and yet we know they are *not* more intelligent than man.

Evolving Spoons. (See fig. #95.)

It is really quite easy to line up any group of artifacts and place them in a sequence to make

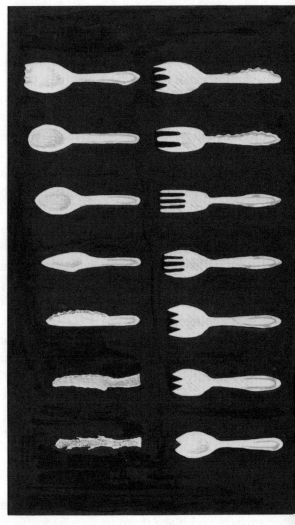

Figure #95. EVOLVING SPOONS

them appear to have evolved. One could arrange utensils from the kitchen in a row and then suggest that the knives evolved into spoons, which evolved into larger ones. Then they involved into forks! But all the utensils were created.

Just because the skeletal remains of a chimpanzee have a few more "human-like features" than the remains of another chimpanzee, that is NOT evidence that the more "human-like" chimpanzee begat humans! No matter how human-like chimpanzee fossils are, they are simply the remains of monkeys, not creatures on their way to becoming human. What is difficult to understand is that we are expected to believe these apes that are now only fossils did amazing things that apes today cannot do. Evolutionism is truly a fascinating "science." Its adherents line up the skulls from fossilized apes and humans and say the evidence is overwhelming that apes evolved into humans. On one side there are the ape skulls, and on the other, the human skulls. Unfortunately, for the evolutionists, no "missing link" has been found. The size and shape of the skeletal remains depend largely upon the individual's age and sex. They are, of course, also affected by the individual's diet, disease, retarded development (either physical or mental), and even by social customs as in the case of the flathead Indians. It is interesting to note that two of the largest skulls known belonged respectively to an idiot and to a U.S. Senator.

As amazing and wonderful as the brain is, it can be deceived and prevent one from seeing truth. However, a person whose brain is short-circuited in this way, must recognize first that he has a heart problem. If a person has no place in his heart for God, a spiritual paralysis of the mind sets in. He is then open to the deception of evolutionism. But the person who invites the Lord of the universe to perform open-heart surgery will have spiritual perception that enables him to see into the lies and deceptions of the evil one.

The stage has now been set. Let's move on to the next act in which one of the worst cases of skulduggery in the history of mankind will be exposed.

PART X
THE FRAUD FROM HELL: RACISM

Chapter 45: Evolutionism: Hindu Hybrid

Chapter 46: Darwin's Delusion

Chapter 47: Hitler and Evolutionism

Chapter 48: Notable Evolutionists Reveal Their Bias

Chapter 49: National Geographic Society and Racism Today

Chapter 50: The Illusionary World of the Evolutionist

Chapter 51: De-volution, Evil-ution and Devil-ution

Chapter Forty-Five

Evolutionism: A Hindu Hybrid

Offshoot of Hinduism.

We think of evolutionism as a modern-day concept. However, it is an offshoot of Hinduism, which began more than a thousand years before Christ. Both Hinduism and evolutionism believe that in the beginning all was one. Then, for no apparent reason, there was a big explosion which brought about the present Earth and all that exists today. The lower forms of life evolved into higher states. Hinduism promotes reincarnation — another explanation of how one life-form, man or animal, supposedly evolves into a higher form. Hinduism postulates that man is evolving into a higher and higher state of consciousness until ultimately he becomes one with the Hindu god, Brahman — Hinduism's impersonal supreme deity.

The Caste System.

Hinduism and evolutionism are both deeply rooted in racism. In the Hindu caste system (hereditary social classes), the highest caste is the Brahman caste. Wouldn't you know it! The Brahman caste is comprised of the lighter skinned people. The darker-skinned are of the lower caste. This is not an accident, for the castes were established along racial lines.

It is apparent what Satan has attempted to do. Taking the different shades of light and dark skin, he has attempted to destroy the symbols in God's Word for good (light) and evil (darkness), knowing all the while that he represents evil and darkness while God represents truth and light.

The darkness that Satan represents has nothing to do with skin color, but Satan has made skin color a way to question the integrity of God and His Word. At the same time he is attempting to remove himself from focus as the supreme source of darkness, meaning deception, evil and wickedness.

The symbols representing truth and evil have been distorted by Satan. He has used every tactic he knows to divide, conquer and enslave man; and to destroy the concept of the absolute truth of good and evil and the symbol for God's light and truth.

A Look into the History of Racism.

About 1600 B.C., the Aryans, an ancient Indo-European people who were fair-skinned, invaded India. They inhabited the land, and began spreading their religion, which became known as Hinduism. The caste system was developed as the conquerors began to subjugate the Dravidians, the descendants of the dark-skinned aboriginal who previously inhabited India. Within the Aryan's religion was a belief that they were the supreme people. They developed a great sense of pride in their Caucasianism (light skin). This satanic perversion further developed after Europeans started traveling the globe. They found it profitable to make black Africans and other dark-skinned people their slaves.

Darwin Gets into the Act.

In the 1800s, there were several new developments with regard to racism. There was a revival of the ancient religion of Aryan nationalism. Secret societies were formed to persecute the blacks, such as the infamous Ku Klux Klan of America. The secular humanist version of racism was evolutionism, which became famous as a result of Charles Darwin and others. Darwin thought the black man was inferior to and less developed than the white man. Being a "scientist," he developed a materialistic allegory to the caste system and reincarnation. Darwin and most of the early evolutionists were blatantly racist. When Hitler came along, he took the pagan religion one step further, attempting to purify the human race from all impure and defective genes through the science known as eurogenics. Today, eurogenics is once again making inroads into the evolutionary scientific community.

Evolutionism and Aryanism Merge.

The movements of evolutionism and Aryanism merged and became the Nazis of Germany. They sought racial purity and Aryan supremacy. Hitler and many of the Nazis were infatuated with ancient Germanic religion and all sorts of occultism. Their caste system excluded the blacks, and the Jews were considered to be the untouchables of India. Hitler often expressed hatred for Christianity, calling it a bastard (illegitimate) Jewish sect. Like a Hindu, he was a vegetarian for religious reasons, and considered the proper treatment of animals one of the highest virtues, all the while killing millions of Jews. Nazism's swastika is an ancient Hindu symbol that was occasionally used by other occult groups.

Evolutionism Merges with the New Age Movement.

Today the New Age movement is bringing back secular evolutionary humanism and Hinduism, declaring that man is god and that there is neither good and evil nor sin. They, too, have a caste system. They declare that there must be a purging of any undesirables (unwanted babies, handicapped, the aged, senile, Christians, etc.) in order that the peoples of the world can live in a state of harmonic convergence ready to evolve into a higher consciousness (nirvana) where all will be one again and all will be good. They, too, desire to purify the human race from all impure and defective genes. They are waiting for the next ascended master (New Age term for anti-Christ) to lead them into the blissful future.

As the Bible points out, this new leader will lead the world into the greatest holocaust the world has ever known. It is easy to see how evolutionism is only an offshoot of Hinduism and how Satan continues to divide and enslave man through his deceptive doctrines and religions.

Spiritual Evolutionism.

Satan's strategy is to convince man that he can become a god. Evolutionists have been duped into thinking that man is simply in a transitional stage. He began as an ape and will end up as a god. Thus, the next stage for man is higher consciousness and higher awareness. They believe that in this stage man can take control of his own evolution. In fact, they believe it is man's responsibility to do so — both individually and corporately. Man may find that to evolve further and reach his New Age potential, a worldwide leader will be needed.

The goal of the New Age movement is not very new: to take man to a new stage of development — godhood.

> Then the serpent (Satan) said to the woman, "You will not surely die. For God knows that in the day you eat of it your eyes will be opened and **you will be like God,** knowing good and evil (Gen. 3:4,5).

Chapter Forty-Six

Darwin's Delusion

(See fig. #96.)
Darwinian Disciples.

Two disciples of Darwin's delusion were Nietche and Carl Marx. Nietche was the father of Nazism, and Marx was the father of communism. Both anti-God religions led to the slaughter of tens of millions and the enslaving of hundreds of millions more with tactics such as fear, force and intimidation.

Evolutionism teaches the survival of the fittest. As a result, war, slavery and racism have been the fruit of its instruction. Evolutionists have taught for years, and even do so today, that the way of man has been a long violent struggle. Survival is supposedly in his genes. They believe it was necessary for ancient man as he was evolving, to seek food like any other creature. Today there is an attempt to improve the image of evolutionism. Some evolutionists claim that

Figure #96. CHARLES DARWIN

the original idea is all wrong and that man wasn't a savage, but a gentle, docile and thick-headed creature. The real savages were the wild beasts in the fields. When and how man supposedly became gentle, no one knows. It is truly amazing the lengths to which evolutionists will go to cover their inhumane tracks, to maintain their anti-God religion, and their public image as a benevolent society with the best interest of all creation at heart. Nevertheless, as much as evolutionists try to cover their past, it is obvious that racism has been promoted through the doctrine of evolutionism.

Darwin's Racist Comments.

The works of Charles Darwin reveal some hideous and blatant racist statements:

> At some future period not very distant as measured by centuries, the civilized races of man will almost certainly exterminate and replace the savage races throughout the world.

It is easy to understand why Hitler relished this theory. This is what led to his view of the superiority of the Aryan race. Darwin continues:

> At the same time the anthropomorphosis (transforming into human forms) apes will no doubt be exterminated. The break between man and his nearest allies (members of the same family) will then be wider, for it will intervene between man in a more civilized state as we may hope. Even the Caucasian and some ape as low as a baboon instead of as now between the Negro or Australian (aborigine) and the gorilla.

This is an incredibly racist statement. In other words, the "superior" races will eliminate the "inferior" ones. The civilized nations will destroy the savage nations. The result of such racist statements were the gas ovens of the Nazis and the present day abortuaries around the world. It puts the black person with the gorilla and the white man as a descendent of a much more civilized creature. Why don't we hear about this side of Darwin from the evolutionary community?

Chapter Forty-Seven

Hitler and Evolutionism

(See fig. #97.)
Hitler was an Evolutionist.

Hitler used the German word for evolution (der Entwicklung) over and over again in his book. In fact, it is not unreasonable to suppose that the very title of Hitler's book *My Struggle*, was influenced by Darwin's subtitle, *Struggle For Existence*, and by the German supporter and defender of evolutionism, Ernst Haeckel, publisher of a book in 1905 entitled *Der Kamkpf Um Den Entwicklungs-Gedanken* (*The Struggle Over Evolutionary Thinking*).

Is it any wonder Hitler was so outraged during the 1936 Berlin Olympics when Jesse Owens, a young black athlete, won four gold medals in the track and field events? It was a humiliation to his evolutionary belief that the white man was far superior to the black man. Hitler congratulated some Olympic victors pub-

Figure #97. ADOLF HITLER

licly some privately, but hastily left the stadium after Jesse Owens won, so he wouldn't have to honor him. Owens was a threat to Hitler's theory of racial superiority.

Darwin's theories also came to be openly publicized in political and military textbooks as the full justification for war. Man was now considered morally right and just. Therefore, he could destroy anything "sub-human" whether man or beast. Highly organized schemes of national policy using the doctrine of force and strength became the dogma of right.

Hitler had little place in his heart for a religion that worshiped a Jew. He rejected the ethic of "loving one's neighbors" as commanded in the Bible and went about slaughtering millions. He attempted to ram "survival of the fittest" down the world's throat. Hitler was a champion of evolutionism. The world today, for the most part, despises him. By way of contrast, Jesus, a Jew, allowed His life to be taken from Him for the benefit of His enemies.

Chapter Forty-Eight

Notable Evolutionists Reveal Their Bias

Edwin G. Conklin.

Two very notable evolutionists wrote on Darwinism before Hitler's rise to power. Edwin G. Conklin, a professor of biology at Princeton University for 25 years (1908-1933) and president of the American Association for the Advancement of Science in 1936, wrote:

> Comparison of any modern race with the Neanderthal or Heidelberg types shows that all have changed, but probably the Negroid races more closely resemble the original stock than the white or yellow races. Every consideration should lead those who believe in the superiority of the white race to strive to preserve its purity and to establish and maintain the segregation of

the races, for the longer this is maintained, the greater the preponderance (prevailing influence) of the white race will be.

Henry Osborn.

Henry Osborn, a professor of biology and zoology at Columbia University and president of the American Museum of Natural History's Board of Trustees for 25 years (1908-1933), wrote:

> The Negroid stock is even more ancient than the Caucasian and Mongolians, as may be proved by an examination not only of the brain, of the hair, of the bodily characteristics ... but of the instincts the intelligence. The standard of intelligence of the average adult Negro is similar to that of the eleven-year old youth of the species Homo sapiens.

In a book dedicated to John T. Scopes, (the evolutionist teacher made famous by the 1925 Scopes Creation/Evolution Trial), *Evolution and Religion in Education,* Osborn wrote:

> The ethical principle inherent in evo-

lution is that only the best has a right to survive...

Missing in Action.

The above blatantly racist statements reveal the hideous nature of evolutionism. The statements were made at a time when little outcry would be made for such demeaning remarks. Today, if anyone in a prominent public position were to be so outspokenly racist, he would immediately be reprimanded and removed. Such was the case with a well-known TV sports analyst and commentator who broadcasted the NFL weekly football games on one of the major networks for years. One day he made an unfortunate statement that contained negative overtures toward black athletes. He was quickly and silently removed from his post, never to be heard from again. The same occurred with a member of President Reagan's cabinet, James Watts, who likewise made an unwise ethnic pronouncement which had racial overtones. Because of Mr. Watts' strong stance for Christian ethics, the news media made a major issue over the unfortunate statement, which led to his resignation.

Today evolutionists are careful to guard against being associated with racism. However, it is clear that racism flourishes in the manure of evolutionism. Charles Darwin spoke of the gorilla and the Negro as possessing evolutionary positions between the baboon and the civilized races of man (Caucasian). Present-day evolutionists, for the most part, do not want to be identified with racism; so Darwin's statements touching on this area receive little attention.

In April 1986, *The Pennsylvania Gazette* (University Of Pennsylvania) published an article featuring a skull labeled "Negro/Lunatic." The caption under the photograph read, "'Scientific' Racism" Skulls like these, housed in the university museum, were once used to 'prove' white supremacy. In other words, during the past, the University of Pennsylvania displayed artifacts which regarded the white man as being far superior to the black man.

Chapter Forty-Nine

National Geographic Society and Racism Today

Dark Skin Implies Primitiveness.

Evolutionism has no other explanation for the development of man's intelligence but a slow progression. This suggests that various groups throughout the history of mankind have emerged with superior intelligence, while others have not evolved as rapidly. Guess what skin color has been considered to be slow in developing? Although it is not specifically stated in the evolutionary charts that those with dark skin are less evolved, it is certainly implied.

A fitting modern-day example of such an inference can be seen in a relatively recent publication of the *National Geographic* magazine. In November 1985, the National Geographic Society set before the public a display of transitional forms which supposedly reveals

"4,000,000 years of bipedalism" — when man emerged from walking on all fours to walking on two feet. Nine "hominids" (man-like creatures) were positioned in line, suggesting evolutionary development. **(See fig. #98.)** Although the article does not state why the earliest figures are darker, it is obvious to the viewer that there is a progression from darker to lighter. The editors acknowledged that the skin color is only speculative. Why is the progression portrayed from dark to light if the skin color is only speculative? Be-

Figure #98. THE EVOLUTION OF SKIN COLOR

GUESS WHICH SKIN COLOR

cause they believe the darker the skin, the more "primitive" the man. This is another example of a subtle form of racism still influencing the public today.

The Bible and Skin Color.

All over the world, prideful men have invented stories to prove superiority over others. Hitler had an illusion that a "pure Aryan race" was destined to rule the world. The Bible has no such fantasies. It asserts that we are all descendants of Noah.

REPRESENTS LESS INTELLIGENCE?

The Christian, as a follower of Jesus, does not have the option of being a racist. Jesus was not a racist. He told His followers to love their enemies, not to kill them. He sought to "draw all men" to Himself (Jn. 12:32). "He made from one, every nation of mankind to live on all the face of the earth" (Acts 17:26 NAS).

Jesus exalted neither white nor black. The Church, the body of Christ, is comprised of people from all races. One of the reasons America has been so strong in the past is because it has been the melting pot of the nations. When cultures come together, they grow stronger. When the Church begins to truly practice loving one another, including those from different cultures, it will become a dynamic force in the world.

Chapter Fifty

The Illusionary World of the Evolutionist

Can a Pig Become an Angel?

There are many atheists who mistakenly regard social and cultural evolutionism as a means by which humans may progress beyond the level of hatred and mistreating their own kind, to a stage of love and respect for their fellowman. This is about as unlikely as a pig becoming an angel. Evolutionists are hoping that although all men descended from an ape-like ancestor, there will eventually be unity and loving harmony among all the various ethnic branches of mankind. Thus, it is believed all humanity may dwell in peace and prosperity — and live happily ever after. Turn on the nightly world news and see how close we are to that 20th century fairy tale!

The Foolish Delusion.

Prominent evolutionary anthropologist, Richard Leakey, expressed irresponsible and illusionary hopes in the concluding pages of his book, *The Making of Mankind*.

> Many people are content to leave their future to the will of God, but I believe this is a dangerous philosophy if it avoids the issue of responsibility. It is my conviction that our future as a species is in our hands and ours only; I would remind those who rely on God's mercy and wisdom of the old adage "God helps those who help themselves." We must see the dangers and the problems and so chart a course that will ensure our continued survival ... For me the search for our ancestors (among the apes — my addition) has provided a source of hope. We share our heritage and we share our future. With an unparalleled ability to choose our destiny, I know that global catastrophe at our hands is not inevitable.

Leakey and Hinduism Go Hand in Hand.

In this naive and absurd appeal, Leakey recommends what is nothing more than a bit of Hinduistic religion. He believes there is more to be gained by looking inward (at oneself) rather than outward (in religion) to another — God. But without a Supreme Authority above man, there is no absolute good nor bad (right and wrong); and hence no reason for an individual to make choices beneficial to anybody except himself.

Within this philosophy, there is no reason to help the poor, the sick nor the starving, which is why India is in such a pitiful state today. In fact, such efforts would be counterproductive to natural selection — the supposed mechanism of evolutionism made famous by Charles Darwin in 1859. According to Darwin, natural selection states that the strongest survive and the weak die out — which is good for the survival of a species. This is Hinduism, evolutionism and a man-centered gospel that was born in hell.

An atheistic evolutionary world view is insufficient to achieve the worldwide unity that Leakey and other evolutionists expect. Only true Christianity based on biblical creation, including the message of redemption, can provide a common physical and spiritual bond for all mankind, both for the present and for the future. The bond Christians share in the Son of God transcends blood relations (Matt. 12:48-50), and all the varied groups of humanity (Gal. 3:28).

The Future of Man Via Evolutionism.

What you believe about your origin is extremely important to your welfare. **(See fig. #99.)** When a society believes that evolutionism is true, then evolutionism becomes the foundation for determining the value of an individual. If a person does not measure up to the standard, then he can be experimented on, or even eliminated.

Figure #99. FORMING THE FUTURE OF MAN

This is why evolutionism is so dangerous. It promotes abortion and racism. There are evolutionists who actually believe that human development must be controlled to help remove genetic flaws within mankind. They want to prevent weaknesses from being passed on to future generations. Eugenics is the study of the control of human heredity, and is directly related to evolutionism. Adherents want to obtain control of those considered inferior or genetically weaker to prevent endangering the quality of life for future generations.[42]

Evolutionary Death Camps Await Man in the Future.

It is obvious that the modern evolutionary community has tried to cover the inhumane racist tracks left by the early evolutionists. They are suggesting that ancient man was really a gentle creature. The bloodthirsty savages were really the wild four-legged beasts in the fields. But the same savage and inhumane spirit remains in the evolutionary dogma. It is hidden beneath the sophisticated and deadly lie that man must protect his species from genetic contamination in order to save himself from extinction. This leads to genetic engineering, euthanasia, infanticide and abortion. It also leads to government control of the children, the aged, the sick, the handicapped and any other group within society that could cause problems, including religious groups like Christians who don't agree with such control. It is a venomous lie that was birthed in the pit of hell. This lie is in direct opposition to the Word of God.

The Bible strongly objects to genetic manipulation. Fifty years ago there was a political group called the Nazis who gained control of Germany. They believed the lie of evolutionism and decided they would produce a "superior race." They began to separate the people into groups — those who were superior and those who were inferior. Those who were inferior were isolated and placed in work camps, and many millions were murdered in concentration camps. The future of man, if evolutionism has its way, is doomed. Without God, only evolutionary death camps await us.

Man didn't evolve from a beast, but many have become beasts. Values clarification has come to the American public school system because of the evolutionistic teaching that we are the result of an accident rather than the creation of an Almighty God.

Chapter Fifty-One

De-volution, Evil-ution and Devil-ution

Should We Be Surprised?

Each day in the U.S. public school system, 6,250 teachers are threatened with injury and 260 are assaulted. There are 100,000 students who carry a gun to class, and 13% of gun incidents in the public school system involve elementary-aged students. Why should we be surprised, for we read in the book of Hosea 8:7:

> They have sown the wind and they reap the whirlwind.

It is not surprising that our young people act like animals since they have been taught they come from them. Animals live for three reasons:
1. Self-propagation
2. Self-preservation
3. Self-gratification

We have a generation of young people who do the same. Evolutionism teaches man is an accident rather than an incident and that a person is no more valuable than an animal. It teaches man is a happenstance, and when a person believes that, it affects the way he lives.

Lovers at First Sight.

Hitler, atheists, and evolutionists were lovers at first sight because they all believe that "might is right" and do not believe in God.

If there were no God, then man really would be a product of pure chance and a descendent of the animals. There would be no intrinsic difference between man and animal other than man's being more intelligent and therefore able to control the animal world. Man would be different only by his intelligence.

Pet Lovers and Beef Eaters.

Evolutionists, then, believe that man is superior to animals only because of his superior intelligence. Yet they believe man has the right to control and even to kill less intelligent creatures.

Man can eat fish, chicken, beef, kill a mosquito, a pesky fly, or a malaria germ, have a pet dog, bird or some other creature — even a monkey. He has the right, because he is more intelligent, to do whatever he wants to the less intelligent creatures. Now you can understand Hitler's thinking was merely practicing the basic evolutionary premise that intelligence and might make right. In other words, the stronger have the right to subjugate the weaker.

Stalin, Hitler, and other modern-day dictators and the evolutionary community all have the same belief system. First of all, they believe there is no Creator God. Secondly, they believe man is a product of blind chance and is no different than any other animal, except he is more intelligent; therefore, he has no intrinsic value. But according to the Bible, man is totally separate from the animal world and does have intrinsic value. He is made in the image of God, not a beast.

De-volution, Evil-ution and Devil-ution.

As long as evolutionism and its denial of God is alive and well, we are only a hop, skip and a jump from the same kind of inhuman, abominable treatment of humans as we saw with Hitler. Such atrocities are in fact happening today in aborturies around the world, and now with euthanasia — the killing of the aged.

Just as we put our pets to sleep when they are old and sick, so it will be with the elderly who are weak and sick. Evolutionism and the Hitlers go hand in hand. This is the de-volution of man. It is evil-ution at its worst, and devil-ution — or hell on earth. Without God, atheism is suicide. On the other hand, God gives meaning and hope to life.

PART XI
THE BIBLICAL PERSPECTIVE OF MAN

Chapter 52: The Truth About Fred Flintstone

Chapter 53: Dead Men Do Tell Tales

Chapter 54: The Genesis Man

Chapter Fifty-Two

The Truth About Fred Flintstone

(See fig. #100.)
The Life and Times of Fred Flintstone.

Most everyone has heard of Fred Flintstone, his friendly neighbor, Barney, and his pet dinosaur, Dino. Although Fred is only a cartoon character created in Hollywood, he has been helpful in the public's acceptance of the caveman myth: that the rise of civilization has been a slow and arduous journey through eons of time. It teaches that man slowly evolved from a marauding troop of cavemen to our present-day civilized and cultured society. From their primitive beginnings, man has become refined, polished and more intelligent than ever, and is now ready to lead us into a glorious future. Such a fantastic notion just does not line up with the evidence.

The Truth About Fred Flintstone

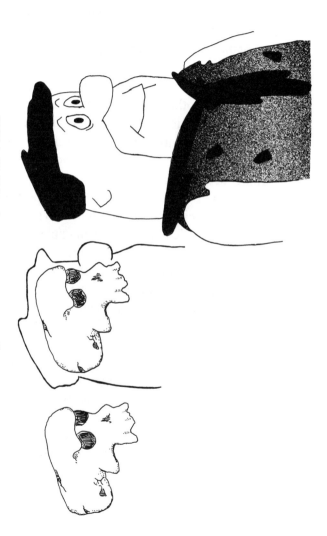

Figure #100. THE EVOLUTION OF FRED

The Explosion of Civilization.

Archaeologists find that human culture has not evolved through successive stages from the days of the cave-dwelling Flintstones to nomadic hunters to farm village dwellers and finally, to builders of great civilizations. Instead, the evidence reveals the sudden appearance of advanced civilizations without signs of a slow evolutionary upward climb from primitive cavemen. The evidence fits the biblical account. According to the Bible, man was created in the image of God; he did not evolve from ape-men. The older the civilization, the more mysterious, the more fantastic and the more unexplainable it is — if one believes in the evolutionary model of man. Archaeologists have discovered that civilizations came suddenly on the scene.

For instance, they have found very few historical roots for the great civilization in Sumeria.[43] Archaeologists have uncovered a civilization fully developed right from its beginning. The Sumerian civilization **(see fig. #101)**, one of the oldest discovered, is located in the Mesopotamian River Valley (the Garden of Eden). These people had metallurgy, art, the potter's wheel and writing. They lived in a highly developed state.

The evidence for a slow development of the

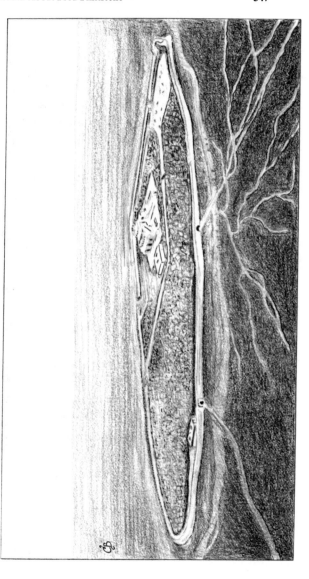

Figure #101. THE SUMERIAN CIVILIZATION

Flintstones and their ape-men kin to civilized man as evolutionism proposes is totally lacking in archaeological evidence. However, the evidence does fit the biblical record for the origin of ancient civilizations. Early in the Bible, in Genesis 4, development of cities and of technology, art, metallurgy, domesticated animals and musical instruments is recorded.

The Cradle of Civilization.

Archaeological research has confirmed the biblical account of man's origin and development, which is another striking testimony of harmony between science and Scripture.

The Garden of Eden was situated somewhere within what is known as the Fertile Crescent — Mesopotamia (present-day northern Iraq). **(See fig. #102.)**

Genesis lists 15 geographical facts about the Garden of Eden. Eleven of them are written in the present tense, which reveals that the writer of Genesis was speaking of a real place. The entire book of Genesis (except chapter 49, which is prophecy) is a book of historical facts. Adam and Eve were as real as people living today. Adam is mentioned nine times in the New Testament, while Eve is mentioned four times. Each reference speaks of them as actual people (I Tim. 2:13; I Cor. 11:9).

The Truth About Fred Flintstone

Figure #102. THE CRADLE OF CIVILIZATION

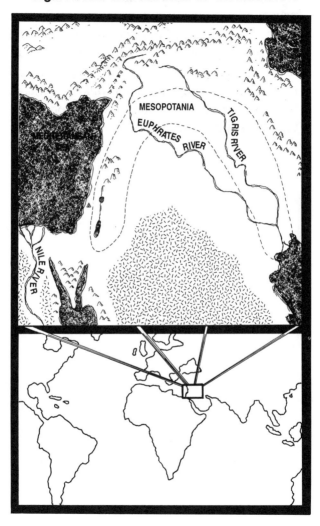

There is so much evidence for the origin of man coming from this region, as recorded in the Bible, that there can be no doubt regarding the accuracy of Scripture. Science has truly confirmed the historical reality of Genesis and the location of where the first man walked on planet Earth. Fred Flintstone, Barney, evolutionism — they all make us laugh.

Chapter Fifty-Three

Dead Men Do Tell Tales

Out of the Past.

Today we know that the stories of people can live on thousands of years after they have long since become dust. Autobiographies, audio and videotapes allow us to take a look into the lives of people long after they have died. But even before books and electronic recordings were invented, man left his story on rocks and caves and in tombs and ancient monuments. Today, through the science of archaeology, we are uncovering stories of people and of whole civilizations that have been buried in the dust for thousands of years. Dead men do in fact tell tales — tales that add to the crushing weight of evidence which continues to mount against the myth of evolutionism and literally buries it in the dust of the ages.

Apes from Man.

A new, unbelievable theory is arising from within the evolutionary community. Evolutionists are now conjecturing a new call of the wild. They are asserting that apes may have evolved from humans! The way each succeeding generation of humans is outdoing the previous one with its decadent behavior, they may be on to something! **(See fig. #103.)**

How is it that all evolutionists are looking at the exact same evidence, yet believe two completely opposite theories regarding the evolution of man?

The reason is simple. Two totally erroneous and contradictory conclusions can be reached from the same set of evidences if all the scientists begin with a wrong basic assumption — one that is contrary to biblical truth. Once fossil evidence is viewed in the light of creation, the contradictions quickly clear up. However, the evolutionists' new view is in some ways closer to reality than they realize. The way of man is not up, but, tragically, down. Man is becoming more and more decadent.

Another Look at Archaeology.

Why are there still primitive groups of people living in countries that are advancing in

Dead Men Do Tell Tales

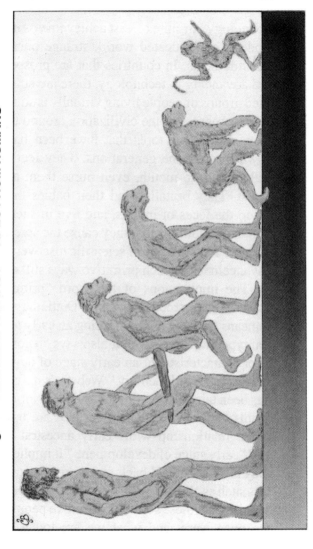

Figure #103. A NEW FANTASY — APES FROM HUMANS

technology? In spite of vast achievements in our modern, sophisticated world, strange phenomena still exists. In countries that are prospering and advancing in technology, there are still isolated groups of people living virtually untouched by the progress of the civilization around them. They use simple tools that have been handed down through the generations. They feed animals mouth-to-mouth, even nurse them at the breast. They brutally bind their babies' heads, tattoo the faces of infants, and live in such unsanitary conditions that they cause the spread of disease. Why in a day of scientific discovery and advancement do such primitive ways still exist?

The implications of the word "primitive" must be understood. Webster's Dictionary says it means "closely approximating an early ancestral type: little evolved." It also says "belonging to or characteristic of an early stage of development; crude, rudimentary." Webster's definition has been tainted by evolutionary bias. Notice the words "little evolved" and "crude" are used in direct relationship with "early ancestral type" and "early stage of development." It implies that they have been held back by environmental factors such as climate, poverty and disease. In other words, what these so called primitive people are, we once were, and what we are today, these primitives will inevitably become.

Let's take another look at the evidence and see if it doesn't reveal the opposite to be true — that man is not ascending up the ladder of civilization from once a primitive past but in actuality, he has been descending from his magnificence at creation.

The Mayans.

The Lacandon of Central America, descendants of the Mayans, today live in very primitive conditions. The Mayans were once a glorious civilization. The ruins of hundreds of cities reveal this incredible fact. From 1500 B.C. to 900 B.C., the nation flourished. Their astronomers kept an accurate record of the movement of the planets and stars. Their mathmeticians gave us the concept of the zero. The Mayans were intellectual giants of Central America.

But the walls of the ruins reveal moral decay — human sacrifice to the Mayan gods. To appease their gods, they slaughtered people by the tens of thousands. Explorer Cortez found a decadent society when he observed the Mayans in 1570. Thus, we see achievement, then moral decay. Their descendants aren't "primitive," but are decadents of society. The Mayan people have not moved upward, but downward in a long and tragic descent.

The Incas.

The Catcheas of Peru are the descendants of the once proud, glorious and magnificent Incas. Today many are addicted to cocaine, which destroys the mind and leaves the people numb, with little or no motivation.

The Incas were one of the greatest civilizations of the past. They were noted for their organization and engineering. They built one road over 3,000 miles long. The Incas constructed with such precision that no mortar was necessary, and many of their ancient structures still stand in place in spite of the many earthquakes that have occurred over the centuries. Their water system lasted for centuries, and is still intact today.

Skulls from Peruvian burial grounds reveal bone regeneration following surgery. The Incas were performing bone surgery — before the time of Christ! The instruments they used are successfully utilized by surgeons today.

Machu Pichu, a masterpiece city, was made of stone which was quarried in a gorge and somehow transported up thousands of feet to the top of the mount; there it was used to build palaces and temples. But like so many other cities in ancient Peru, Machu Pichu had torture chambers and places to make human sacrifices.

As powerful as the Inca civilization was, corruption from within destroyed it.

The List Continues ...

There are many other civilizations that rose to a peak and then came to a sudden end. Egypt was the land of the Pharaohs and boasted of the world's first centralized government. Babylon contributed to the development of the sundial, the potter's wheel, the dome, the arch and the vault. Phonecia was a nation of commerce and a source for the English alphabet. Greece was the birthplace of democracy, the land of Pathagres, Socrates, Plato and Aristotle.

The Lie of Ever Onward and Upward.

Why would civilizations rise to such heights only to suffer collapse? For many centuries the collapse of civilizations was attributed to moral and spiritual decay. However, within the last hundred years, a new line of thought has emerged. Some are suggesting that other reasons — plagues, changes in trade routes, agriculture depletion, earthquakes, disruptive changes in environment or famine — caused the collapse of civilizations.

Natural disasters and economic reverses can indeed cause problems, but if a nation is internally strong, these problems serve to strengthen it. However, if the civilization is bankrupt spiritually, the least adversity will cause it to topple. The idea of an ever onward and upward progression of humanity to new heights of glory is not borne out in history, Time is not the savior, but rather the destroyer.

The Truth of the Matter: Degradation.

Man, created with a free will, chose to disobey God and surrender his will to Satan. It was man's sin that caused the whole creation to fall from its original perfection. Death and decay was introduced for the first time, and the harmony of nature was distorted. The further man became separated from the Garden and his Creator, the more degraded he became. Degradation and degeneration continued through subsequent generations. That is the truth of the matter. Evolutionists hold to the belief that the future of mankind is onward and upward toward a state of moral, physical, ethical, social and mental perfection. However, history tells us that just the reverse is true. When man loses touch with the Creator, Who is the source of all truth, his mind becomes darkened and his ways become evil. The more evil a man grows, the more "primitive" he becomes. Thus, being "primitive" is a result of the moral and spiritual degeneration of a group or nation of people. There are people today living "primitive" lifestyles in caves, who left civilization to get back to "nature." They have simply rejected science and technology to live a life free from restraint.

Whenever there is moral and spiritual degeneracy, the result will be decadence and eventual collapse. Empty cities are the result of empty lives, and the aftermath of a pagan society whose people know not their Creator. But there is a cure: a return to God.

Chapter Fifty-Four

The Genesis Man

(See fig. #104.)
Made in the Image of God.

> Then God said, "Let us make man in our image, in our likeness, and let them rule over the fish of the sea and the birds of the air, over the livestock, over all the earth, and over all the creatures that move along the ground. The LORD God formed man from the dust of the ground and breathed into his nostrils the breath of life, and man became a living being (Gen. 1:26; 2:7).

The Bible is the key that unlocks the mystery of ancient man. It portrays man as a creature made in the image of God — with tremendous intelligence and the ability to perform great accomplishments. The Bible portrays ancient man

Figure #104. THE GENESIS MAN

as having superior knowledge to man today (Eccl. 1:9 LB). Keep in mind that science and technology are an extension of Christianity. They are a result of the reformation — a time of great awakening to God and His Word, which opened the door for the advancement of the sciences. Man was in touch with reality, with his Creator God and His creation rather than with Satan through pagan worship, superstition and myth.

Coding the Original Man.

When God created man, he was made with godlike attributes and capacity. Man was coded with complete wisdom and knowledge from the moment of his creation. This does not mean he was omniscient, but that he was fully functional within the context of his environment. He was instantaneously mature and complete — like a living cell, which is fully functional at the moment of division. Man was coded with the ability to appreciate and understand the laws of nature. In the next volume of the Creation Science Series — *The Original Man and His Amazing Achievements* — we shall take a look at what the Bible says regarding early man — Adam and his early descendants. We shall investigate the incredible and astounding evidences around the world which confirm the truth of Scripture that original man was not a primitive half-breed, but an incredible creature made in the image of God. He had knowledge superior to that of man today and the ability to construct incredible structures around the world. Indeed, early man was no savage caveman; he was the capstone of God's creation.

The Conclusion

Kicked Out of the Kingdom.

The ABCs of evolutionism have truly made a fascinating fantasy, one that was fabricated in the pit of hell. Satan has been telling the only kind of story he knows how to tell: a lie. Created as a beautiful and perfect being, he was kicked out of God's kingdom because of his rebellion. Since that day, he has been trying to climb back out of the pit in which he found himself. Unfortunately, the way for Satan is not up; it's down. He will continue on his path downward towards destruction and judgment. Until that day, his alphabet, his devilish doctrine, will continue to be taught and will be embraced as truth by those who, like Satan, are intoxicated with the delusion of becoming God. They will hold on to evolutionism as their security blanket, in hopes that it will keep them safe. But when the day of judgment comes, their security blanket will do them no good.

Missing Links Still Missing. (See fig. #105.)

Meanwhile, if humans had evolved from apes millions of years ago, there would be hundreds, if not thousands, of missing links or tran-

Figure #105. MISSING LINK STILL MISSING

sitional forms between man and apes. How strange it is that after more than 100 years of searching for fossils of such creatures that they have been unable to find anything but a couple of fragments that are on the evolutionary charts as possible suspects.

It must be remembered that the evolutionists who attempt to fill in the gaps between man and ape from fossil fragments do so with an evolutionary bias. They have preconceived fantasies which dictate how the remains are reconstructed. It is all nothing more than science fiction at its worst.

Man was created a fantastic being. All the evidence reveals this to be the case: the Bible, archaeology, history, legends and the traditions of ancient man. Evolutionism is the myth which supposes that life arose by chance from inanimate chaos to produce intelligence and design. One can visit every major museum in the world and not find the missing link because it just doesn't exist.

A Sad End for a Deceived Distinguished Gentleman.

I began this book recounting Walter Cronkite's interview with two of the world's leading anthropologists. Cronkite, a world famous journalist, was the host. He was attempting to confirm evolutionism with these prestigious visitors. However, the interview turned into being more of a monkeyshine and tomfoolery show as his guests ended up arguing among themselves as to the more correct view for man's origins. I am concluding this volume with a final excerpt from another evolutionary program also hosted by Walter Cronkite. Mr. Cronkite narrates the newly released four-part documentary titled *Apeman*. The video series was of the finest professional quality. Its purpose was to reinforce the ape-man theory. This program was produced many years after the account shared in Chapter one, as Cronkite has continued his search for his roots through evolutionism. However, at the end of the series Mr. Cronkite concludes with this incredible remark:

> "I came to Africa to find my ancestors.
> I don't know if I found them."[44]

This is astounding since the four hours are dedicated to documenting and proving that man's ancestors are the apes. He opens up the video by reading Genesis 1 on the creation of man. He openly rejects the biblical creation story and proceeds to try to find his origins. He then concludes that he still doesn't know if he found anything to substantiate his personal beliefs. One should reject evolutionism on logical grounds alone. There just is no evidence to substantiate its claims.

Theological Reasons for Rejecting Evolutionism.

Not only should evolutionism be rejected on logical grounds, but for theological reasons as well. H.G. Wells stated in *Outlines of History:*

> If all animals and man evolved then there were no first parents, no paradise, no fall. And if there had been no fall then the entire historical fabric of Christianity, the story of the first sin the reason for the atonement collapses like a house of cards.

He Wasn't Even a Christian, But He Was Right.

Evolutionists believe all we humans need is a little boost to get over the problem of doing wrong. They think that by removing an evil person from his environment and putting him in a nice one, he will be transformed.

Christians on the other hand, believe that man needs a birth from above to get over the problem of sin. Change a man within and the environment won't matter — even if he is on death row at the state penitentiary.

The first creation was easy for God; He simply spoke it into existence. The second crea-

The Conclusion

Figure #106. BECOMING A NEW CREATION

tion or the new creation was much more difficult. It required that He hang on a cross and receive unspeakable torture mentally, emotionally and physically. But He was willing to endure the pain because of His incredible love for us! A person can choose to become a new creation by accepting Jesus Christ as Lord and Savior. Or he can choose to believe the myth of evolutionism that says man is a descendant of the apes. What will you do? **(See fig. #106.)**

Endnotes

1. *Dallas Times Herald* (Thurs. April 1984).
2. *Bible-Science Newsletter* (May 1974), p. 6.
3. *"Science, God and Man,"* Time Magazine, (December 28, 1992), p. 4.
4. H. Bleibtreu, *Britannica Book of the Year*, (Chicago: Encyclopedia Britannica, Inc., 1985), p. 163.

    R. Leakey, *The Making of Mankind*, (London: Michael Joseph, Ltd., 1981), Chapters 13 and 14.
5. B. Rensberger, "Ancestors — A Family Album," *Science Digest*, Vol. 89, (1981), pp. 34-43.
6. Duane T. Gish Ph.D., *The Amazing Story of Creation*, (California: Institute for Creation Research, 1990), pp. 77-90.
7. Dr. Alex Hrdlicka, *Ancient Remains of* p. 495.

8. Sir Arthur Keith, *Antiquity of Man*, (London: 1925).

9. W.A. Criswell, *Did Man Just Happen?* (Michigan: Zondervan Pub., 1993), p. 120.

10. R.B. Goldschmidt, *The Material Basis of Evolution*, (New Haven: Yale University Press, 1940), pp. 84-98.

11. *Ape-Man Videocassette Series Documentary* — 1994, A & E Television Networks Hearst/ABC/NBC.

12. *Ape-Man Videocassette Series Documentary* — 1994, A & E Television Networks Hearst/ABC/NBC.

13. *ABC-TV*, (Australia: October 14, 1993 and April 2, 1994).

14. Martin Monestier, *Human Oddities: A Book of Nature's Anomalies*, (New York: Citadel Press, 1990).

15. *Nature*, 77:587, (1908).

16. Sir Arthur Keith, *Antiquity of Man*, (London: 1925), p. 159.

17. Noah's Flood and the Ice Age are covered in Volumes V and VI of the Creation Science Series.

18. *Dallas Times Herald*, September 26, 1991.

19. *Early Man*, Time Life Nature Library, (New York: 1968).

20. *National Science Foundation Lecture Series*, Notre Dame University, (March 1971).

21. S. Code, *Leakey's Luck*, (1975), p. 297.

22. An extinct species of early man who is said to have some advanced human-like characteristics and who is supposedly dated about 1.5 million to more than 2 million years old.

23. Volume IX of the Creation Science Series, *The Dismantling of Evolutionism's Sacred Cow — Radio Metric Dating (RMD)* takes an in-depth study of the weaknesses of radio metric dating.

24. John Reader, *Missing Links: The Hunt for the Earliest Man*, (London: Collins, 1981).

25. Boisei was added to this fellow's name; named after Charles Boise — a supporter of Louis Leakey who described and named the original finds.

26. Dr. Oxnard, *Fossils, Teeth and Sex*, (1987).

27. Dr. Solly Zuckerman, *Beyond the Ivory Tower*, (1970).

28. John Reader, *Missing Links*, (London: Collins, 1981), pp. 9, 73-110.

29. *Ape-Man Videocassette Series Documentary* — 1994, A & E Television Networks Hearst/ABC/NBC.

30. *National Geographic*, (April 1979), and *Science News*, (February 9, 1980).

31. *Dallas Times Herald*, (February 4, 1980).

32. Such tracks are discussed at length in Volume VII of the Creation Science Series, *The Dinosaur Dilemma: Fact or Fantasy*.

33. Library of Curious and Unusual Facts.

34. *The Dallas Morning News*, (May 9, 1994).

35. *Time Magazine*, (November 7, 1977).

36. Cover Story, *Discover*, (September 1986).

37. *National Geographic*, (June 1973), Highlighted by *NG*.

38. *National Geographic*, (June 1973), Highlighted by *NG*.

39. *Newsweek Magazine*, (March 29, 1982).

40. *The Dallas Morning News*, (January 23, 1982) Section 2A.

41. Erhard Winkler, op cit.

42. J. Crow, "The Quality of People: Human Evolutionary Changes," *Bioscience*, (1966), pp. 16:863-867.

    F. Osborn, "A Return to the Principles of Natural Selection," *Eugenics Quarterly*, (1960), pp. 7:204-211.

43. Clyde R. McCone, *Symposium on Creation IV*, (Michigan: Baker Book House, 1972), pp. 123, 133.

44. *Ape-Man Videocassette Series Documentary* — 1994, A & E Television Networks Hearst/ABC/NBC.

Bibliography

Ailleo, Leslie. *Discovering the Origins of Man.* Great Britain: Stonehenge, 1982.

Amazing Prehistoric Facts. New York: Millard Press, 1991.

American Museum of Natural History. *The First Human Origins.* New York: Harper Collins, 1993.

Bliss, Ed.D., Richard B. *Origins: Creation or Evolution.* California: Master Books, 1988.

Baugh, Ph.D., Carl E. *Panorama of Creation.* Oklahoma: The Southwest Radio Church, 1989.

Bowden, M. *Ape-Men: Fact or Fallacy?* Bromley Kent: Sovereign Publications, 1977.

Caird, Rod. *Ape-Man — The Story of Human Evolution*, MacMillian Co. 1995.

Clark, Harold W. *Fossils, Flood, and Fire.* California: Outdoor Pictures, 1968.

Clayton, John N. *The Source: Eternal Design or Infinite* Accident? Indiana: Superior Printing, 1976, 1978.

Coffin, Harold G. *Creation-Accident or Design?* Washington D.C.: Review and Herald Publishing Association, 1969.

Creation Ex-Nihilo. *Ancient Civilization and Modern Man.* Australia: 1995.

_____. *Any Little Green Men Out There?* Australia: 1993.

_____. *Aborigines Knew About the Flood.* Australia: 1991.

_____. *Aborigines Technology vs Evolutionary Racism.* Australia: 1992.

_____. *Comet Collision Coming.* Australia: 1994.

_____. *Darwin's Bodysnatchers.* Australia: 1992.

_____. *The Fossil Record.* Australia: 1987.

_____. *Genesis and Evolution Don't Mix.* Australia: 1987.

_____. *The Human Fossils Still Speak!*

Australia.,1993.

_____. *Iceman Found in Glacier.* Australia.,1992.

_____. *Little Known Facts About Dead Apes.* Australia: 1986.

_____. *National Geographic and the Stone Age Swindle?* Australia: 1986.

_____. *That New "Missing Link."* Australia: 1995.

_____. *No Bones About Eve.* Australia: 1991.

_____. *That Pig of a Man Didn't Fool Everyone!* Australia: 1991.

_____. *The Roots of Modern Racism.* Australia: 1990.

_____. *Why the Electric Battery Was Forgotten.* Australia: 1994.

Creation Ex Nihilo Technical Journal Vol.6 (Part 1). Australia: Creation Science Foundation, Ltd., 1992.

Discover. *Almost Human.* Chicago, IL: 1990.

_____. *Baffling Limb on the Family Tree.* Chicago, IL: 1986.

_____. *Facing Up to Man's Past.* Chicago, IL: 1983.

_____. *The Great Leap Forward.* Chicago, IL: 1989.

_____. *How to Read Ancient Menus.* Chicago, IL: 1982.

_____. *Hard Evidence.* Chicago, IL: 1992.

_____. *The Iceman Cometh.* Chicago, IL: 1992.

_____. *Old Bones Week.* Chicago, IL: 1984.

_____. *We First Stood on Our Own Two Feet in Africa, Not Asia.* Chicago, IL: 1986.

_____. *Women of the Year: The Old Girl Network.* Chicago, IL: 1988.

Dixon, Dougal. *After Man: A Zoology of the Future.* New York: St. Martin's Press, 1981.

Dougherty, Dr. C.N. *Valley of the Giants.* Cleburne, TX: Bennett Printing Co., 1971.

Gish, Ph.D., Duane T. *The Amazing Story of Creation from Science and the Bible.* El Cajon, CA: Creation Research, 1990.

———. *Evolution: The Challenge of the Fossil Record.* El Cajon, CA: Creation Life Publishers, 1985.

———. *Evolution — The Fossils Say No!* San Diego, CA: Creation Life Publishers, 1973.

Gowlett, John. *Ascent to Civilization — The Archaeology of Early Man.* New York: Alfred A. Knopf Inc., 1984.

Green, John. *On the Track of the Sasquatch.* Agassiz, British Columbia: Cheam Publishing, 1968.

———. *The Sasquatch File.* Agassiz, British Columbia: Cheam Publishing, 1973.

———. *Year of the Sasquatch.* Agassiz, British Columbia: Cheam Publishing, 1970.

Hill, Harold. *From God to You by Way of the Zoo.* Old Tappan, NJ: Fleming H. Revell Co., 1985.

Huse, Scott M. *The Collapse of Evolution.* New York: Baker Book House, 1983.

Kohahl, Ph.D., Robert E. *Handy Dandy Evolution Refuter.* San Diego, CA: Creation Science Research, 1977.

Lambert, David and the Diagram Group. *The Field Guide to Early Man.* New York: Facts on File, 1987.

Life Nature Library. *Early Man.* New York: Time-Life Books, 1970.

_____. *Evolution.* New York: Time-Life Books, 1964.

Lubenow, Morvin L. *Bones of Contention: A Creationist's Assessment of the Human Fossil.* Grand Rapids, MI: Baker Book House, 1992.

Monestier, Martin. *Human Oddities. A Book of Nature's Anomalies.* New York: Citadel Press, 1978.

Morris, Henry M. and Gary E. Parker, *What is Creation Science?* San Diego, CA: Creation Life Publishers, 1982.

Morris, John D. *Noah's Ark and the Lost World.* El Cajon, CA: Master Books, 1988.

McLean, Dr. G.S., Roger Oakland and Larry McLean. The Bible Key to Understanding — The Early Earth. Eston, Canada: Full Gospel Bible Institute, 1987.

National Geographic. *Ethiopia Yields First*

"Family" of Early Man. Washington, D.C.: 1976.

_____. *The Ice Man: Lone Voyager From The Copper Age.* Washington, D.C.: 1993.

_____. *The Leakey Tradition Lives On.* Washington, D.C.: 1973.

_____. *The Search for Modern Humans.* Washington, D.C.: 1988.

_____. *The Search for Our Ancestors.* Washington, D.C.: 1985.

_____. *Skull 1470.* Washington, D.C.: 1973.

Nelson, Byron. *After It's Kind.* Minneapolis, MN: Bethany Fellowship Inc., 1967.

Oard, Michael and Beverly. *Life in the Great Ice Age.* El Cajon, CA: Master Books, 1993.

Parker, Ed.D., Gary E. *Creation: The Facts of Life.* San Diego, CA: CLP Publishers, 1980.

Richards, Lawrence. *It Couldn't Just Happen.* Fort Worth, TX: Sweet Publishing, 1987.

Saint, Phil. *Fossils That Speak Out, Creation vs Evolution.* Greensboro, NC: Saint

Ministries Int'l, 1985.

Science News. *Skulls Give Hominid Evolution New Face*. Washington, D.C.: 1986.

Segraves, Kelly L. *The Way it Was*. San Diego, CA: Beta Books, 1976.

Tanner, Jerald. *Views on Creation Evolution And Fossil Man*. Salt Lake City, UT: Modern Microfilm Co., 1975.

Tattersall, Ian. *The Human Odyssey*. New York: Prentice Hall General Reference, 1993.

Time Magazine. *How Man Began*. New York: Time Inc., 1994.

Time Frame, *The Human Dawn*. New Jersey: Time-Life Books, 1990.

Watson, David C.C. *The Great Brain Robbery*. Chicago, IL: Moody Press, 1976.

_____. *Myths and Miracles, A New Approach to Genesis 1-11*. Worthing Sussex: Henry Walter Ltd., 1976.

Weister, John. *The Genesis Connection*. Nashville, TN: Thomas Nelson

Publishers, 1983.

Wilder-Smith, A.E. *Man's Origin, Man's Destiny.* Minneapolis, MN: Bethany Fellowship, 1975.

List of Graphs and Illustrations

1. Evolutionism's Wildest Guess: Taking a Second Look 7
2. Are You Related to Adam or Apes? 12
3. The Great Debate: Who's King of the Mountain? 14
4. The Imaginary Ape-Man 16
5. The Differing Human Prehistoric Time Line Theories 20
6. The ABCs of Evolutionism and the Road to Monkeyland 23, 24
7. The Changing Face of Evolutionary Creatures 26
8. Tabloid Tales of Ape-Men 28
9. Alien Evolutionism 33
10. Ape-Man Family Tree 41
11. Amusing Evolutionary Ape-Men 42
12. Unholy Inspiration 43
13. A Typical Evolutionary Chart 46, 47
14. Glaring Gaps of Evolutionism 48
15. Evolutionary Tree of Death 49
16. The Empty Coffin 50
17. The Last of the Missing Links 53

18.	The Original Missing Link	55
19.	Amoeba to Man	57
20.	The Missing Chain	59
21.	The Meager Evidence	63
22.	Retirees from the Original Cast	65
23.	Hindu Ape God	66
24.	The Real Ramapithecus	69
25.	The Ape-Man Syndrome	73
26.	The Missing Link — Always Looks the Same	74
27A.	How to Fabricate an Ape-Man	78
27B.		79
28.	Before and After	80
29.	Filling in with an Imaginary Mind	81
30.	Java Man	84
31.	The Missing Pieces	85
32.	A Pronounced Proboscis Possession	87
33.	Where in the World is Java?	88
34.	The Passing of Java Man	91
35.	Nebraska Man	93
36.	The Cusp of Hesperopithecus	95
37.	Family Portrait	97
38.	The Passing of Nebraska Man	100
39.	Peking Man	102
40.	Peking Puzzle	104
41.	The Passing of Peking Man	107

List of Graphs and Illustrations 387

42.	Piltdown Man	109
43.	Piltdown Puzzle	110
44.	Filling in the Imaginary Lines	112
45.	Will the Real Piltdown Skull Please Emerge?	113
46.	The Implements of Crime	114
47.	The Passing of Piltdown Man	120
48.	Mr. Neanderthal	125
49.	Home Sweet Home of the First Missing Link	126
50.	Mr. Cool Dude	128
51.	Ape-Man or an Elderly Person?	129
52.	The Homes of the Neanderthal Race	130
53.	Skeletal Diseases/Rickets — Normal	132
54.	A Case of Neurofibromatosis	134
55.	Cro-Magnon Man	137
56.	Neanderthal's Relatives	138
57.	Neanderthal's Face-Lift	141
58.	Caveman Art	144
59.	Marquis De Lafayette	145
60.	The Iceman	148
61.	Homo Sapiens Not Homo Simians	153
62A.	Your Order Please: Sapien or Simian	154
62B.		155
62C.		156
63.	Skull 1470	161
64.	Beauty or Beast Depends on the Artist	164

65.	Australopithecus	177
66.	400-Piece Puzzle: A Cranium Crack-up	180
67.	Will the Real Mr. Z please Stand Up?	181
68.	Ape-Woman of the Year	185
69.	Lucy's Remains	186
70.	Pygmy Chimpanzee	188
71.	Lucy's Measurements	190
72.	Fossil Footprints	202
73A.	Next Door Neighbors: Dinosaurs and Humans	205
73B.		206
74.	Ancestral Worship	209
75A.	A Rare Genetic Miscue	225
75B.		226
76.	Bigfoot: Fact or Fantasy?	235
77.	A Living Fossil	238
78.	Twenty-first Century Cavemen	248
79.	Comparative Anatomy: A Look at Apes and Man	255
80.	Linking Chickens to Chimpanzees	256
81.	Four Hands or Four Feet?	258
82.	Quadrupeds: Four on the Floor	259
83A.	Looking at the Lineup	260
83B.		261
84.	Sizing Up the Brains	263
85.	They Must be Relatives	264
86.	Big Toe Baloney	270

List of Graphs and Illustrations

87A.	Miss Pitifulcus: Only Her Hairdresser Knows	273
87B.	....	274
87C.	....	275
88.	The Marks of Man	277
89.	Any Art Ain't Ape-Man Art	280
90.	The Roots and Fruits of Evolutionism	289
91.	Ancient Indian Customs	295
92.	Foreheads Fool Sages of Science	296
93.	Modern Man Head Shrinkers	301
94.	Who Came from Whom?	306
95.	Evolving Spoons	308
96.	Charles Darwin	319
97.	Adolf Hitler	323
98.	The Evolution of Skin Color	330, 331
99.	Forming the Future of Man	336
100.	The Evolution of Fred	345
101.	The Sumerian Civilization	347
102.	The Cradle of Civilization	349
103.	A New Fantasy — Apes from Humans	353
104.	The Genesis Man	361
105.	Missing Link Still Missing	365
106.	Becoming a New Creation	369